D1046256

"Curious about what other retirees are doing with themselves after they say goodbye to their mid-life careers? *Shifting Gears* reveals the rich abundance of retirement ventures, from the exotic to the mundane. Don't count on a sure-fire retirement recipe with the baby boomers. Our generation is making retirement challenging, fun, relaxing, invigorating, contemplative or all of the above. *Shifting Gears* will whet your appetite with first-hand tales of retirement so varied your head will spin."

> — Sara Zeff Geber, PhD, Author, *Essential Retirement Planning for Solo Agers*

"In *Shifting Gears,* Richard has written a helpful guide for modern retirement – that is staying active, redefining goals, and just about anything other than riding off quietly into the sunset. They're deeply personal tales about cultivating meaning. The wisdom in these pages helped me realize our golden years could be our best chance to understand ourselves, live exactly how we want, and maybe even do something amazing."

> — Matt Fuchs, Journalist covering healthcare and aging news, *Washington Post* contributor

"Retirement – it's a stage of life that many people dream of. Often marketed as a time of rest and relaxation, Richard Haiduck helps us discover this period can be definitely something else. By sharing real stories, he demonstrates how retirement is truly a unique and personal journey. From asking questions about life to filling time with passion and purpose, Richard dismantles the idea that retirement should ever be experienced from a rocking chair."

> — Susan Williams, Founder, *Booming Encore*, a top ranked website and influencer for baby boomers, aging and retirement

"In short, fast-moving interviews Richard Haiduck paints 50 pictures of the surprising and interesting ways people successfully transition from working for a living to living after working. The individual pictures create a bigger canvas; a montage that captures the spectacular richness, diversity, courage, generosity and curiosity of the human spirit and how that spirit can express itself in a new phase of life. I thoroughly enjoyed *Shifting Gears* – it made me think about my upcoming shift."

> — Daniel G. Welch, Author, *Race for the Mind*, a highly rated novel about an Alzheimer's patient and the quest for a cure

"Striving! Arriving! Now What? Where to begin. The inspiring and encouraging stories in *Shifting Gears* offer a kick start to the next journey."

> — Rick Eigenbrod, PhD, Author, *What Happens When You Get What You Want?*

"*Shifting Gears* is a unique, fascinating look at retirement and aging. Told by retirees between the ages of 50 and 102, the stories weave a consistent theme of choice, which often is a 180-degree turn from career days."

> — Carolyn Berry, Author, *Adventures with Grammy "How To"* series and the upcoming *Adventures with Grammy: Let's Explore the Mid-Atlantic*

SHIFTING GEARS

50 Baby Boomers Share Their Meaningful Journeys in Retirement

RICHARD HAIDUCK

© 2020 Richard Haiduck
All rights reserved.

No part of this publication in print or in electronic format may be reproduced, stored in a retrieval system, or transmitted in any form or by any means, electronic, mechanical, photocopying, recording, or otherwise without the prior written permission of the publisher.

The scanning, uploading, and distribution of this book without permission is a theft of the author's intellectual property. If you would like permission to use material from the book (other than for review purposes), please contact the publisher. Thank you for your support of the author's rights.

Editing, Design and Distribution by Bublish, Inc.

Photo courtesy of Santa Clara University

Hardback ISBN: 978-1-64704-243-1
Paperback ISBN: 978-1-64704-226-4
eBook ISBN: 978-1-64704-244-8

Contents

Prologue

Winding up from the picturesque village of Conques in the south of France is the Le Puy route of the iconic Camino de Santiago pilgrim trail. The Peregrinos (pilgrims) who have chosen this part of the route face one of the steepest climbs on the five-hundred-mile trail. The trail at this point is a narrow gulley surrounded by forest, and it winds upward through a series of switchbacks. The peak can't be seen, so it creates uncertainty about whether you have enough reserves to make it to the top. There are loose rocks underfoot; it's easy to misstep, especially after fatigue has set in. It's only natural to lower your head and watch your step to avoid a fall.

Rounding one of the switchbacks, you emerge from the dense tree coverage and suddenly realize you have made it. You've arrived at the peak.

There, in the clearing, you see a surprising object: an oval-shaped wooden outhouse. Scrawled across the door by a grateful Peregrino are words you will remember for the rest of your life: "Lift up your head, the hard part is over." You have arrived at the peak and have earned the right to lift your head and enjoy what you have accomplished.

Many of the stories in this book are about people who can lift up their head. They have completed a lot in their life; a big part of their climb has been accomplished They have earned the right to lift up their head for this next stage of their life. They are deciding what is important to them and making choices. Some of those choices are challenging and aggressive, but they are being done as a matter of choice. The retirees have earned the freedom to make choices about what they really want to do next. They tell us their stories in *Shifting Gears: 50 Baby Boomers Share Their Meaningful Journeys in Retirement*.

Shifting Gears tells about the individual shifts made by the retirees as they transitioned into this stage of their life. A downshift for some, an upshift for others, steady cruising for a few. The book is focused on retirees who share stories about their meaningful journeys in retirement.

The stories are a sampling of the broader shift of a whole generation that is reshaping retirement. The boomer generation is taking different approaches to their retirement years; it is nothing less than a generational culture shift. They have more time, more money, and more freedom to do things that the previous generation could not even consider. Their stories demonstrate an attitude, a culture, and a willingness to make new lifestyle choices.

It's not your parents' retirement. We baby boomers are different. We grew up in remarkably different times, and those cultural influences have led to a refreshed attitude toward how we want to spend the rest of our life.

Our parents' generation—what Tom Brokaw so famously called the Greatest Generation—were a group of folks born between 1901 and 1927. They grew up in the Great Depression and fought in World War II. The new technologies of radio and telephone had a major impact on their lives. There was a shift from rural America to urban and suburban living. The times they lived in shaped their character and values. They were known for their persistence and taking personal responsibility. They had a strong work ethic and sense of loyalty.

In 1950, a sixty-five-year-old man had an average retirement of eight years, 45 percent of these men continued to work, and the average social security benefit was $280 per month.[1] The retirement decision was driven by going away from work, rather than going toward some new activity. The retiree had a simple life and lived modestly, usually in the community where he or she had worked. Those of the Greatest Generation are often the parents of the baby boomers.

Our baby boomer generation was born between 1946 and 1964. We grew up in a strong postwar economy and were the first generation to grow up with TV. It was a politically active generation, making important progress in advancing civil rights and feminism. It is a generation that is self-assured and decisive, while at the same time resourceful, competitive, and focused.

According to US Census Bureau data, the average length of retirement is now eighteen years, 20 percent of retirees are continuing to work, and average monthly social security payments are $1,503. In addition, retirees now have Medicare coverage for a large part of their medical expenses. More money, more time, and a generation known for its activism are a powerful combination of drivers for a reinvented retirement.

With those stark differences between the two generations, it's not surprising that our generation is reinventing retirement. Those in our boomer generation are being activists and pushing our limits. We want more—more activity, more passion, more experimentation. No longer is retirement simply ceasing work and adding a leisure activity or two. It's so much more. Giving voice to these changes by sharing

---

[1] Report from the Stanford Center on Longevity, New Realities of an Older America, Adele M. Hayutin, PhD, Miranda Dietz, Lillian Mitchell 2010.

the personal stories of this new generation of retirees shows just how far we've come. We're having an impact on those around us.

Examples show that the stakes are higher. Many of the people who were interviewed for this book have called retirement the best time of their life. It's time for baby boomers to see more examples of what their peers are doing. It's time for other generations to take note of the full social potential of a reinvented and energized generation.

Conversations with fellow retirees first awakened me to the need for giving voice to these changes. Peter left his cushy corporate job in his early fifties to devote himself to climate change. Dave competed in the Senior Olympics in his seventies. Linda retired solo in the foothills in Colorado with her nearest neighbors being four-legged. Rick took a contemplative walk on the Camino de Santiago and reset his priorities. Milt went to Panama and installed artificial hands on amputees. Chuck dealt with the adversity of having his dream house destroyed by a fire. As I had more and more conversations with boomer retirees, my antennae went up. I sought out more stories of what they were doing with this stage of their life. Over time, I recognized a generational trend that couldn't be ignored, and the examples hadn't yet been fully articulated. Embracing a whole new lifestyle by taking on a vibrant range of active, challenging, fun, meaningful, and socially engaged activities in their "golden years" isn't the retirement experience of a select few, but a driving force for this generation.

I became determined to share their stories and awaken us all to the shift toward a more expansive way of retiring that is happening right now. The idea for a book of first-person stories was born. It tapped into my own desire for a challenging and meaningful activity after I stopped working. It stirred my long-dormant desire to be an author.

As a seven-year-old kid, I was certain I wanted to be an author. No doubt about it. Fireman? Test pilot? Those careers had moments of interest, but never rose to more than second choice. My parents got me a writing pad, some #2 pencils, and a much-needed big eraser. I was off and running toward being an author.

The stories were all fiction, and never longer than one page. Pats on the head from parents and teachers gave me plenty of encouragement to continue writing.

Then, after about a year, the writing stopped as quickly as it had started. I was a kid. I changed my mind. There was no precipitating event; other fun kid activities just sort of eclipsed my writerly urges.

The passion to be an author ceased for sixty-five years. I got busy getting an education, having a family, and building a career. Nothing happened on the author front. Life experiences and maybe even a bit of wisdom accumulated. My listening skills evolved and sharpened. These new skills were used in my life, but not for writing.

Now, fast-forward more than six decades, and the idea of being an author hit me like a gust of fresh air. I was invigorated. I would be an author, this time with perhaps more sophisticated tools than the #2 pencils and notepad.

First, I went back to my friends who had originally shared their experiences with me. I recorded our conversations and started asking more questions to get the details and emotional backdrop necessary to show more clearly how they were defying the traditional limits for this stage of life.

After hearing from those closest to me, it was time to hear from people I had never met. The goal was not just to get more stories, but to get stories from a more diverse pool—I needed a range of people with disparate backgrounds and experiences. There are 47 million Americans over the age of sixty-five. Ten thousand more turn sixty-five each day. The average life span is now seventy-nine years. That means there are a *lot* of potential stories to listen to. I focused my search on people who showed passion and a determination to better themselves in this reinvention phase of life. Many pursued activities that made them feel good about themselves, whether it was a hobby, paid work, a volunteer opportunity, more family time, dealing with adversity, or a spiritual exploration.

At first, I leaned on friends for referrals to people who they thought might be willing to speak with me. Building trust with these strangers was critical. I knew that the way I conducted the interview was going to be key to having an open and trusting conversation. Great stories come from spontaneity, so the interview needed to be open and free-flowing, and built on trust.

Terry Gross, the iconic NPR personality was the masterful interviewer who served as a role model to help me refine my skills: Terry knows how to ask short, open questions and begin by encouraging the interviewee to talk about comfortable topics. Only after the interview has progressed and trust has been built does she ask questions like "Oh, really?" or "Why do you think that is?" or "How did you feel about that?" By the end of the interview, people are divulging much more than they would with a more rigid set of questions, and the audience benefits by getting a brighter and clearer portrait of this person in their own words. This was my model.

I began each interview with this open-ended question: "How would you describe this stage of your life?" and that got us off to a good start. Over time, as my interviewing skills evolved, my questions got shorter—and the responses grew more in-depth. I was surprised, and pleased, at how open and trusting these strangers were. I was appreciative of their willingness to share not only their experiences, but their most intimate fears, motivations, and hopes.

One of my first interviews with a stranger was with Donna. She's undergone four leg surgeries and was on a cane for three years. Once healed, she decided to climb Mt. Kilimanjaro, the tallest mountain in Africa. She tested her limits in an unforgettable and inspiring way.

Maurice is a four-time Emmy-award-winning documentarian, who has always worked for someone else. Now he has decided to step out from an employer's shadow and shoot a documentary with his own total creative control. This time he's doing a project the way *he* wants to do it. And he'll do it in Gaza.

Michael has had to deal with breaking up with his partner of twenty-four years while simultaneously losing his vision.

Jane and her girlfriends decided that their seventies were the right time to learn to play the ukulele and share the joy of a new hobby together.

Bruce and Jill have always had a passion for helping people in tough circumstances. Now they both volunteer in a maximum-security prison, teaching anger management to prisoners using Buddhist meditation principles.

The stories just kept coming. This project continued to demonstrate the social trend of a generation setting higher limits for themselves.

The book is a collection of oral histories, using the words of the interviewee describing how they are shifting gears as they move forward in their meaningful retirement journey. Some are shifting smoothly, some grind the gears a bit, and some are still learning to shift. Their stories are a slice of their reality at the moment. Open questions remain in several stories. The reader will get a short but vivid portrait of each person and what they have done, but also a glimpse of the motivations and emotions that have accompanied their activities.

The content of the stories was the selection criteria, rather than the age of the person or what stage of retirement they're in. Each story was selected because it uniquely adds to our understanding of how this generation is dealing with retirement. The reality of their situation is portrayed, with the full range of joy, sadness, inspiration and challenges that they expressed.

Each reader will take away something different from this book. Some of the stories will resonate; some may seem foreign and unfamiliar; others may have less of a connection to the reader's own areas of interest or viewpoint. The goal is that all of you are entertained by these stories and that some of you may find ideas and inspiration to try something different in your own retirement.

You can take comfort in knowing you are not alone in seeking to tailor your life into what you want for these later years. There is a large community of your fellow explorers, several appearing in the following pages.

A Word about COVID-19

Note that all of the interviews were conducted prior to the onset of the COVID-19 pandemic. Clearly the pandemic has had a temporary stifling or delaying effect on many of the retirement activities described in these stories.

Elders have been the most vulnerable to the medical ravages of this disease, because of both our age and the frequency of preexisting conditions. We need to make adjustments to protect ourselves. But our generation has a second unique vulnerability that we often overlook. Our clock is ticking. We have a limited amount of time remaining to enjoy our retirement. And our knees will not be getting stronger, if we've planned to do physical activities.

There is a need to balance the two vulnerabilities and come up with a plan to reopen retirement. Reopening retirement will be a second reinvention for our generation. Some of our plans will need to be modified, and we may need to find new directions. We're the generation of people who've reinvented themselves once before. Now we need to reinvent a second time, and adjust for this new situation.

PART ONE

PONDERING RETIREMENT: THE CONFUSING CHOICES

The last day of work may just creep up on us. All of a sudden, retirement is about us, and not about that other guy. We may have had time to plan in advance, but rarely are all of the uncertainties removed by that planning.

Sometimes retirement leaps out at us, maybe caused by an employer doing a downsizing. Or sometimes there is something in our personal life that causes retirement to become something to consider now. Maybe health-driven. Maybe family-driven. Maybe money-driven.

Whatever caused the retirement decision to be imminent, the subject introduces a whole range of new uncertainties, new decisions to be made, new ways of looking at our activities of daily living. Finishing a career often has an element of letting go, with impact on our identity and our sense of self-worth.

All of these factors add up to retirement day being an emotional time. It's natural for it all to be a bit overwhelming. You've got a lot of choices, and often you have the luxury of trying lots of things and seeing what is best for you.

In this section, we will hear from people who are wrestling with retirement issues and trying to figure out what to do next. It's not easy. You can feel the pain and uncertainty that some may experience. Nobody said shifting gears was always going to be easy. Each of them has put a lot of thought into what is right for them and their family, and are still examining those questions. They don't have all the answers, but they have some good thoughts for us to consider.

TO RETIRE OR NOT TO RETIRE: TAKING TIME TO GET IT RIGHT

"I find myself with the reminder that sometimes it's okay to just hold off on any decisions for a while."

Greg has retired twice, most recently two months ago. His last job was as CEO of a company that distributed good, clean, wholesome videos. That company tried to harness capitalism as a force for good. Greg strove to combine caring and capitalism.

Greg now needs to decide what to do next. He may go back to full-time employment, but he is weighing his alternatives. He wants to get it right, rather than decide quickly. His methodical approach is one of searching for activities that fit with his belief that we are here for a reason. Greg is in the midst of that exploration process.

Right now is a time of discernment, trying to discern what's next, what should be next, if anything should be next, and sort through that. My career has stretched over forty-plus years already. It's almost two months to the day that I had my last day in the office.

There are three very distinct phases that I've noted over these two months. The first, quite frankly, is almost embarrassing to say. It was like a junkie going through a withdrawal, I suppose. We had structured my prior business as a very data-driven business. Every morning I would start my day with review of the past day's performance over a whole variety of data points on dashboards. I literally went through a withdrawal period when that was no longer necessary.

The second phase that I noticed involved my sleep habits. I was typically a six to seven hours of sleep per night kind of guy. I felt I was functioning just fine, sleeping like normal, and one day I realized, man, I just slept nine hours. It was interesting for me to realize that I would wake up after nine or sometimes even ten hours and go, 'Wait a minute . . . *that's* not my norm.'

Now, the third phase is a matter of discernment. It's a matter of trying to discern what it is I'm supposed to do—both from the standpoint of my higher calling and also in my day-to-day activities. I'm just now coming up on sixty, so hopefully I still have plenty of years and days ahead. What am I supposed to do with that? That's the stage that I'm in at this moment.

I'm trying hard not to rush it. There were very few gaps of employment in my forty-something years. There was always the next step well in sight. Now there isn't. I'm trying to just say, 'That's okay.' I don't have to make a quick reaction. Before, I was always of the opinion 'It's better to make a decision now. Change it later if you learn it's wrong.' I find myself with the reminder that sometimes it might be okay to just hold off on any decisions for a while. See how it evolves.

I've spent a fair amount of time hiking, flying, visiting with some friends; and there's been much more grandson time. He's a two-year-old, and the time with him has been just a hoot and a half! There's a pretty big 'honey-do' list that I've been working on. If you'd asked me five years ago, I'd have said my current activities are exactly what I would've wanted to do with this time. The question I need to discern is if we're put here for a reason and there's something more to be done.

The capitalistic world is under severe criticism right now. The world's talking about socialism and democratic socialism. I realized a couple years ago that I truly believe capitalism is the best system that we've got out there. Part of the experiments of my past four or five years have been to show that a business can actually operate as a business, make decisions as a business, check all the discipline boxes of the business, but also find ways to do good.

An outlet that we developed for that was the idea of 'cause marketing.' In the past year, my company was able to help almost a dozen couples adopt a baby by helping them reach their funding goal. More importantly, in the process of channeling cash donations that got them over their funding goal, we also used the tools of our trade, which are audio and video media. We captured their message, their struggles, their stories, and shared them with millions of people on social media to raise awareness of their need for adoption and how other people can make a difference. It was a marketing play that worked really well, but a very collaborative model. It also got babies adopted. That was a pretty cool thing in my career.

Part of my mind is: 'Okay, is there something about my former career that still can be shared or developed further that can make a difference—something I can do rather than just hiking and playing?' I've got half a dozen things on my list right now that I think are interesting to look at and consider.

I'm a general aviation pilot. I will have taken the steps necessary to get my instructor's license and spend more time flying, with the goal of introducing more people to the thrill and the joy of general aviation. One of the things I've done in the past is work with an organization that sponsors something we call Young Eagles Flights. It's all about getting twelve-to-eighteen-year-old kids into small airplanes. You put a teenager in the right-hand side of a small airplane and you go fly over their community and school. The joy that you see spread across those kids' faces is just a big, big thrill. My wife and I have supported one of the community colleges with an aviation scholarship. Introducing more people to aviation is one of those things on that list I am moving forward with.

I grew up Catholic. I consider myself a practicing Catholic and yet I'd never actually sat down and read the Bible until about a year and a half ago. I'm on my second trip through. When you reread, you find you're highlighting different passages because they speak to you at different times based on what you need at that point. That discipline of a daily read has been a very comforting way to enable this intentionality, this slowness, and it reminds me that there's a bigger picture here. It's okay even if the result of that bigger picture is to just go spend time with your grandson.

That daily reading, which I'd never done intentionally until just the past year and a half, is a big part of the peace and the patience that allows me to say it'll come. We should let it happen. Be intentional, be open to it, study, do all the work. This isn't just sitting back and watching TV and seeing what happens. This is discerning what will lead to the right thing at the right time.

2

DEALING WITH CONFUSION: SORTING OUT THE RIGHT PATH

"Meaningful work to me is a super-important part of my life."

Confusion, confusion, confusion. Nobody said this stage of life was going to be simple, or very clear. Suni has a lot on her plate. What must she do to get a start-up off the ground? At the same time, how can she continue making progress with the social enterprise that she operates? Her rewriting of her own retirement is a blend of diverse projects, each with its own set of challenges and opportunities.

Despite the confusing activities, Suni is developing a path forward. She has done it before. She starts with a candid assessment of what is important to her, and then evaluates her alternatives in that context.

think that this generation is rewriting retirement. There's got to be room somewhere in the workforce for our generation, because our generation is active and physically aware and plugged into the universe. We're not like, 'I can't wait until I retire and then I'm going to sit on the porch on a rocking chair.' I'm a baby boomer who wants to lead. All my life I've been involved in social movements and things like that. The idea of volunteering at the soup kitchen seems to me like I'm limiting myself.

I'm used to making a decision. I'm used to creating new things. I'm published. I've done things with my life and a lot of other people have too. I've got to keep going.

This stage of my life is more confusing than I expected it to be.

I'm happy. I'm proud of my life. I feel like I've lived life with integrity, and that is important to me. But I thought things would be more settled than they are.

I was given the opportunity to take an early buyout from the university where I worked, and I hadn't been anticipating retirement for another five to eight years. That meant that zero brainpower had gone into retirement plans and what I'm going to do. I have been saving a little bit of money, but it's not a financial issue as much as it is the other issues that come along with this.

The last time I applied for a job outside of academia had to have been about thirty years ago, and it's not the same. It's like, 'What do you mean, *Indeed.com*?' I also felt like I was too old to be hired, so it wasn't a very encouraging process.

I didn't realize ahead of time that it's not just about stopping working or where you're going to get an income or what you're going to do with your day. It really changes your lifestyle. Do I continue to live in San Francisco—because it's expensive to live here—or do I go someplace else? Do I move closer to where my children are? I'm a widow and I don't have a playmate, someone to just say, 'Hey, let's just pack it in and travel and do whatever we want to do.'

I need people around. I thought, 'Okay, I'm going to apply for a couple of positions.' I applied for this position that I was highly qualified for. I went through five interviews, and after the fifth interview I thought for sure I was going to be hired, and then I wasn't hired. I thought the only reason I cannot be hired is because of my age. Then I thought, 'What am I going to do? Oh, God, I'm really disappointed. I'm kind of angry, disappointed.'

In the meantime, a friend came to me and said, 'I'm doing this business. You want to do this with me?' I said, 'Sure. Yes, give me something, anything!' It was a start-up and I knew I wasn't going to be paid. I just wanted to work, and I needed to work. Then I got really engaged in that, but the partnership didn't work out. After about four months, we realized we were on different tracks, so we split up amicably.

One of the directions that I wanted to take the start-up in was not of interest to my partner. It's an app to reduce postpartum depression in new mothers, because there's just not enough help for mothers right now.

We talked and I said, 'Fine, that's going to be my new company.' So about six months ago I started this company. Everything has a huge, *huge* learning curve. Developing an app is a whole different ballgame than what I'm used to. This is in technology, which I'm not very well-informed about. I'm not a dinosaur but I'm not a technology person either.

I'm bringing this thing forward and I'm in a real stymied place at the moment because I have everything ready to go to the developer. But I'm having trouble getting funding for the development. I have to raise forty thousand dollars, and I don't have forty thousand to put into it.

I don't have a cofounder, and that really makes it hard. I don't have someone with skills that I don't have to flesh out the rest of the company. I do not have all the skills a company like this takes, and I don't have the money to hire people. I've spent a ton of time on it and taken it as far as my capacity will allow.

If I had a cofounder, I would absolutely take it forward. If I had money to build the app, I would absolutely take it forward. If I had money to do a marketing plan, I would absolutely take it forward.

It's not a closed chapter, but I have just shifted it to the back burner, because I don't know where to go with it. I don't know how to get out of my situation. I don't know . . . Maybe it's dead, maybe it's not dead.

In the meantime, I am teaching a few college courses. If I teach a couple courses a year as an adjunct, financially I don't have to tap into savings. I managed to get some courses for the fall and the spring, and that'll carry me through.

I love teaching: I love the work. I love the science. I love the research. I love teaching students and mentoring. I was totally in love with my job. I could do that and that would buoy me through, but there's something in me that wants more. I'm used to a more powerful position than that.

I set up a nonprofit, but it was always secondary to my job. It was based on helping communities in developing countries to do something about reducing parasites. I started the Dragonflies project by going to Vietnam alone and interviewing sixty-seven farmers. I learned about their perception of their conditions and health and what their biggest health problems were. I analyzed the responses and then I created the Dragonflies program.

I trained health advocates from each village about specific behaviors, how to treat your water, where to defecate, dental hygiene, child malnutrition, and keeping the animals out of the kitchen.

My outlook on the Dragonflies program is confusing because that's something I could do. It's something I'm interested in doing, but I don't want to have to give up my life in order to do it. If I really embrace the Dragonflies project and try to make that bigger, it means moving overseas, and I don't want to do that.

Something that might relieve some of the confusion about

Dragonflies could be finding a way to make it possible that I could get some money out of it to live on. It doesn't have to be a high salary or anything. That would be one thing, and then I could devote my time to it but also be able to live in America most of the time. I don't mind making a huge trip a year to all the Southeast Asian countries.

I have no intention of dropping Dragonflies. I will continue doing what I've been doing. I keep looking for a successor, but so far I haven't found one. I always saw Dragonflies as a piece of my life, but not something so all-encompassing.

It's important that I not feel erased. Meaningful work to me is a super-important part of my life. Getting the confusion resolved soon is important to me because I'd like to have an income. The other part of the hurry is this: I sit here and work at home. I work a little bit in coffee shops. I'm alone too much. I have a pretty good social life but I don't have coworkers anymore. I'm used to having a very peopled life. My life is shrunken in that respect. It's hard for me to keep my motivation up when I don't have that connection with people.

If either one of those things—the app or the nonprofit—was a larger organization, I would have coworkers. I would have a cofounder. I would have people I could work with, people to bounce ideas off of. You motivate each other. You push each other. You don't want to let the other person down, so you work harder.

I feel like there were times in my life that were much harder than anything I would ever face right now. In some ways, it's like this isn't life-or-death. I divorced my first husband when I had three babies and no education and went back to school. That was big. If I did that then, I could do this now. In that respect, this is minor.

I'm serious about it, but it's a lot more like playing because I don't know the outcomes. I don't know what's going to happen. I don't even know where to set my goals sometimes or how to achieve them.

As a result, I don't set the goals, which leaves me in even more of a confused quandary here.

Taking care of myself starts with me making my best self. Making sure my attitude is clear. Making sure I am living a healthy lifestyle and I am maximizing my energy and my sense of who I am.

I think we look back at what the things were that helped us the most when we were in difficult situations. With me, it's perseverance and defiance. A lot of people have told me, 'Oh, you can't do this. You can't do that.' I've been like, 'Oh yeah? Well, I'll show you.' I had a teacher who told me I couldn't get a doctorate because I wasn't smart enough. I had three babies at home while I was doing this. Well, maybe getting my doctorate was because I had three babies at home and had nothing to do with my brain!

3

FINDING YOUR RETIREMENT FREEDOM: PUTTING YOUR CHOICES IN PERSPECTIVE

"You can lift up your head now; the hard part is over."
- Sign at the top of a difficult climb on
Camino de Santiago in Spain

Rick is seventy-eight and working part time, but thinking full time. He is a trained psychologist and a keen observer of human behavior. He still does executive coaching that is aimed at people who are in transitional stages of their careers. He uses his quiet time to develop a viewpoint on life. What's the best way for one to own their life? Rick's insight has deepened after two contemplative walks on the Camino de Santiago in Spain and France. He uses his time to think about this stage of his life and how to impart lessons to others. His observations are engaging, at times complex, but they always provoke thought in a way that may help others rethink their own retirement.

U p until now my life, like lots of our lives, has been scripted for me in broad terms. This script or map has been: go to school, then you will get the right job and you will live happily ever after. That script sets up a set of expectations that most of us just aren't even aware of. You know, this is what you do because everybody else is doing it. I think one of the hallmarks of that state is we are really playing a role in somebody else's narrative.

We're rewarded handsomely for it. We're rewarded with certain currencies that we are told are the right currencies: status, money, et cetera. For me, one of the hallmarks of the transition at this age is that that script runs out on us. We don't run out on it, it runs out on us. 'Happily ever after,' we come to realize, is a certain kind of illusion. We've fooled ourselves and the narrative has set us up to do that. That's part of growing up. Each one of us begins to, A) be aware of and then, B) question the narrative and how we are playing our role in it. It begins with awareness because you can't change what you're not aware of. We begin to question it a little bit. We begin to wonder if we own our life or if the narrative owns us.

At the same time, our age has played a part. Our circumstances have played a part. Somewhere around forty or fifty is where we begin to say, 'Wait a minute.' There's a point at which we say, 'The dream that I've dreamed has come true . . . But now what?' or 'The dream that I dreamed hasn't come true . . . And now what?' Regardless, there's probably a need to redream the dream.

The dream of happily ever after runs out on us. It's like, 'What you got for me *now*?' The answer is: 'Not much.' There has been a convergence of age and stage.

Taking a several-day walk on the Camino de Santiago in Spain helps you to think through these life issues. You train up, you fill your backpack, you get on a plane, you land, and then someone drops your ass off at one end of the Camino and you walk to the other end.

Your brain shifts to 'less' because you've stopped the noise. You've stopped all the external stimulation. All the things that had required your attention are gone. The scarcest resource we have is our attention. Out on the Camino, there's less of a demand on your attention, which means your mind gets quieter. What does that result in? How about the cliché, 'being in the moment.' The nature of the physical challenge and the environment you're in forces you to pay attention. To just pay attention. Because you can stumble, you can fall, you can accidentally do all sorts of things.

Through the physical you are drawn to a state of meditation. There's a quietness that comes. Being in the present creates a new attitude. Guess what? It makes spaciousness, not just space, but spaciousness inside of you for things to come, and they do. Spaciousness allows for important information to reach you. It doesn't provide you with *where* to go, necessarily, but with ways of going about getting there. Not a destination, but a direction. It provides you with navigational tools.

Sometimes your thoughts are triggered by something outside of you, and sometimes they come from inside of you. You have no control over it, but you put yourself in a circumstance where you take yourself out of life as you know it. It makes space for other possibilities. There's a term we use when walking this trail: 'The Camino provides.'

I remember at one point, when I first did the walk across Spain, this guy we met said, 'Hey, you want to know how the first presidential debate went?' We went, 'No. I don't want to know about that.' Why? Because it's going to get in my head. I don't want that shit in my head. I can't do anything about it. I'm going to grind about it. Both my buddy and I had an immediate reaction: 'No, I don't want to hear it.'

Both in that journey across Spain, which was seven years ago, and in this one, there's something about walking. Somebody said it's muscle pace. You slow down. You slow down, you slow down, you slow down. Certainly in the first journey, stuff came out of me from nowhere that I didn't understand.

Walking across Spain, there's a section that takes you a week or more to walk across. It's dead flat and I found it boring as shit. I hated it. My buddy loved it. Why? Because there's no distraction. I'm walking across this with Michael, and we're talking and I just said, 'You know, Michael, I need to apologize. You've been hearing me tell stories, and I'm telling you stories about all this shit I did. I'm sorry. I've been a bore.' As I'm telling him this, I start to sob. I start to sob. Do I have a clue what I'm sobbing about? No. I'm not crying. I'm not weeping. I'm not teary. I am sobbing. Sobbing and walking. What occurred to me a half hour later is that I was telling *myself* the story of my life and owning it in a way I never had. It's like I'm talking about some other guy, but no, this is me, I'm that guy.

There was this integrative process of owning my life that I think is a part of this transition that we make at this age. To re-own our lives, to own our lives at a different deeper way than just a bio. Michael said to me at one point, 'I think some of the people here are walking to find who they are. We are walking to affirm who we are.' I think that affirmation process is a possibility at this transitional stage because the noise has reduced for us.

My recent walk on the Camino was way harder than my walk of seven years ago. It was still roughly the same distance, but the degree of difficulty was greater. Just to give you an example, my previous walk was a total ascent of 27,000 feet. Total ascent on this one was 67,000 feet. It's really hard.

There's this one grade that was just a bitch. It felt straight up, and it went on and on and on. It was just grind and grind and grind. You got to the top, and of all things, there was an outhouse there. On this outhouse, in French somebody had written, 'You can lift up your head now, the hard part is over.'

What struck me is that there are three levels to that. One is for this walk, just coming up the hill, the hard part's over. Lift up your head, see what you've earned, see the vistas. Because when we struggle, whether we're walking up a hill or not, the effort brings our heads down. We are invited in this transition to lift up our heads, the hard part is over.

Second, it was the realization that we were not quite halfway through. The most rugged terrain was behind us. Interestingly enough, as you get closer to the end, it gets easier. I went, 'Rick, the hard part's over, lift up your head.'

Third, I realized that's true in my life. The hard part is over, lift up your head. The kids are gone. Financially, we're fine. I love the woman I'm with. I get to live where I want to live. There ain't nothing I need to do. I get to live life as I say. This part of the transition is to be the mapmakers. We have to essentially pick the tools. We have to pick the pieces that guide how we go, not just where we go. We have the choice. We can figure out where to go or we can figure out how to go.

I set my criteria. I don't care what anybody else thinks. I've got to have a design where I get to design my life at this age and stage. I get to write the narrative, and the narrative I'm writing now is always evolving. One of the things that I came back with is a reminder that I don't have to have all the answers. It's about going. How you're going to go is way more important than where you're going to end up.

Since I've been back, the quality of my work, the impact I'm having, and the feedback I'm getting is even more positive. I'm having more fun. It's not that conscious. It's not a sense of I'm doing things differently in some conscious way. When I came back I had this instinct that said, 'Leave space, create spaciousness, see what comes.'

That's just thrilling to me. I'm not scared about it because I can lift up my head, the hard part's over.

For most of the folks that are going to read this book, the hard part is over. Lift up your head. Quit worrying. They can do any goddamn thing they want. The problem is they don't know what they want and they can't tell their wants from somebody else's. The question 'What do you want?' is one of the hardest questions you can ask. Does it come from inside and something natural or is it a habituated want? In this transition, we have a chance to crystallize that, test it out, challenge ourselves. I think I want this.

You're born with freedom. You will die with it. It's not freedom *from*, it's freedom *to*. Freedom's just another word for knowing you can choose. At our age, how conscious are we that we can choose and choose and choose? That's thrilling if you allow it to be, or it is overwhelming if you allow it to be.

At this age, we really have choices, which we're not used to. That's a part of the difficulty of the transitions. I get to do what I want to do because I say so.

Designer life. I get to design my life. That's the prize. That's the challenge. I think we are more at liberty to be designers than we've ever, ever been. We also come back to meet our developmental flat side. We have an opportunity to grow ourselves in a place that might not have been developed.

I want to die with the most me. That's the organizing principle. It's a constant discovery process. It's a constant running up against my own personal boundaries, my big developmental flat side. I want to die with the most me. That informs my choices in some way. Do I think there's going to be a way to have more me come up against my flat side, have some insights, make some shifts? Do I think in part by walking I'm going to get that? I can't guarantee it, but my experience says yes.

17

This is maybe just saying the same thing in different words. We are gifted with this problem. It's a gift. We are lucky. We have earned it. We have been given this problem. Lift up your head and see the gift. The hard part is over.

4

TRANSITIONING FROM FIRE CHIEF: FINDING A NEW BALANCE

"The fire station still contacts me for my opinion."

Dan retired three months ago from his position as fire chief. He is in the midst of a transition to new activities. His lifelong commitment to service has guided his choices regarding what comes next.

would say I'm still in a flux. It's still confusing to me. I always thought I'd be retired about this time, and I had plans to retire, but it's a learning curve. It's still confusing and I've been retired now for three, four months, and I'm still learning. I even tell people, 'I'm not sure I'm retired yet, because I think it's almost like this long vacation and that I'll be going back to work eventually.'

I do a lot of work around the house, little things that I haven't been doing for the last twenty-five years. That's been nice.

Every day, I have a plan, in the sense that I tell myself, 'I'm going to go do this tomorrow.' And that's when my wife Judy says, 'Are you going to *stop*? Are you going to sit down for a minute?' I say, 'I don't know how to stop. I'm getting there. I'm getting there, trying to relax.' I don't want to sit around and do nothing. That's my biggest fear.

I've been teaching at College of San Mateo for almost twenty years. Just part time, teaching the Emergency Medical Technician class. When they got wind of me retiring, the director of the program asked me if I wouldn't mind teaching some fire science courses. That was a big, 'Oh good, now I can retire because I've got something to do still.'

I love teaching. That's been my one saving grace in the sense that I've truly not retired, because I don't know that I can ever *retire*-retire.

Being a mentor to the students is exactly what I want to be doing, because I have a passion for the fire service. My belief is: it is a public service.

I have five children. They all live at home still, because they can't afford anywhere in the Bay Area yet. They're all home. I've actually had more time with them now than I have in years past. I'm getting to know the kids again. I hate to say it that way, but it is true. Yes, I'm getting to spend a little time with them, getting to enjoy them some more. That's probably the best part of retirement. It's being able to spend more time with the family.

I'm happy with what I'm doing. As Chief, I burned out. There's no doubt about that, that I was physically worn down. I feel healthier, I feel more relaxed today, rid of stress, and I want to stay in that mode. I should be able to get to that point where I'm not stressed always, so I don't want to overcommit. At the same time, I do want to stay busy. I don't want to be the guy sitting on the recliner watching TV.

The nice part is pretty much that I can walk away from anything I've recently taken on. If it's getting to me, I can walk away and not worry about it.

I'm still young. That's one thing about fire service, you get to retire young, but unfortunately, in the case of a lot of folks, you're not retiring healthy. That's what I was approaching. My health is getting better now.

Looking forward, my one worry is my health. I guess if there's something that worries me, it's that I want to be there for my family. I don't mind if I die when I'm eighty, but I don't want to die when I'm sixty. I have a lot to do still. There's a lot I want to do.

5

WINDING DOWN THE WORK: RAMPING UP THE FUN

"From now on, it's going to be more fun for me."

It's time. She's earned it. Time to move on to taking care of herself. Deb is just getting started in this transition from total immersion in her own business to a more relaxing next stage of her life.

I would describe this upcoming stage of my life as something I'm looking forward to. For thirty-four years, I've sacrificed my personal life a lot for my business. I work with physicians and practice management. They're very demanding but I love them to death. I always say I'm like a mama bear protecting her cubs. They work a lot so they expect me to as well, and so I'm always available. It's a rewarding career. I loved it, but I've given a lot. It's really time for me to slow down a little bit.

I'm making a transition to not working as much, to just choosing the projects that I really want to work at. For the first time in probably twenty years, I actually fired a client. Now I can pick and choose the projects that I want to work on.

Managing retirement is going to be easy. Seriously. I think that retirement is sometimes easier for women than it is for men. My male clients have a lot harder time with it because their identity is so caught up with their occupation—being a doctor. My identity isn't totally caught up in my work. Deciding to make this change now was not difficult for me emotionally.

I know what I want because I've been preparing for it for a long time. Every single morning now, I get the paper, make myself a cup of coffee, go in the hot tub, and read the paper. It feels really good because I'm starting out my day in a real positive way.

One of those things that I want to do in my semi-retirement is work in a winery. I just want to pour wine and talk to people. I'm Midwestern. I'm friendly. I've been to almost every state and so I can use that as a conversation starter.

I want to take one month a year and trade my house for someplace else in the world. I want to get involved in community service. I'm redecorating the house. My plan is to do more exercising, including Pilates and riding my bike around Napa.

I'm throwing a 'Welcome to Medicare' party at the end of this month. I have an invitation that says, 'We're having early bird cocktails for those of you who have to go to sleep.' I'm trying to make fun of aging by doing this crazy party.

I've got lots of ideas of what I want to do next. The only problem is that I would love to find a great guy to share this with. I've been so busy I never usually have time to meet people. I want to take a little bit more thoughtful approach to finding a guy. I met almost all my boyfriends dancing. Maybe I should think about some other criteria. I'm being funny, but it's sadly true. It's so hard when you're my age to meet people. It really is. On the other hand, I don't really mean to get married again. I'd like to be in a nice relationship. Somebody to travel with, somebody to do stuff with on weekends. Unfortunately, there are no single men my age in Napa. They're all married. I swear to God!

I figure I've only got twenty more good years. I better make the most of it. I don't have any health problems except I just got braces. I think this is weird, that I'm going on Medicare but I'm like a teenager and have braces.

My biggest unknown is probably my health. It's the only thing that I worry about. Other than that, I think life is an adventure and I'm just going to keep adventuring from here on out. I look forward to it. I'm not fearful of it.

6

STEPPING OUT OF THE MILITARY: ADJUSTING TO CIVILIAN LIFE

"I think I was driven by purpose for so long, and you can say the Army gave me a mission. I think it makes you lazy in figuring some things out. Now, you have to figure out what works best for you."

John has just completed twenty-eight years of military service, which included multiple combat assignments. He has identified some important changes he needs to make in adjusting to civilian life. He paid attention to how best to adapt his military demeanor, his self-reliance, and being home regularly. He is now transitioning from military to civilian life. For his last assignment in the military, he took a position that would give him an early taste of the transition.

He and his wife have carefully planned the economics of the transition to give them the freedom of making choices without having to worry about money. Decisions about his daily activities are now guided by finding something he enjoys and which still has purpose, rather than being just about making money.

The catch phrase for this stage of my life is 'transitional.' For me, it's a lot more stable than my previous stage of life. I am not gone at somebody else's whim anymore. I was very much here and gone based on whatever the government and my training officers needed.

I think veterans miss the mentality that we're used to being around every day. I will tell you we are not like most of society. Generally speaking, we work in an environment that is very much blunt and gruff by its very nature. For sure, that was the case in the part of the military that I was in, the Special Operations community. Blunt and to the point is faster and more efficient in terms of communications. So that's what we do. I don't have to worry so much about people's feelings in the military because there is a hierarchical structure of rank and experience. There are a number of things people just understand when they are a part of that environment. I didn't have to justify my authority. I didn't have to justify my experience base for an opinion. People automatically understood when getting my point of view.

We really don't worry about hurting people's feelings. We really don't worry about other people's opinions. I think part of it is just the environment overall that veterans miss and they feel lost when they leave it.

Once you leave the military environment, you have to figure out what works best for you. What worked for me, what I wanted to do, I thought I'd figure it out for myself.

I think my wife and I have had to figure out what it's like to be in the same space more than we ever have in the past. Part of it was because I was gone a lot in my job—not just day-to-day, but deploying for chunks of time. Now I am here all the time. I think it took us a while to figure things out, occupying the same space as much as we do now.

The times when I was gone could be as short as three days at a time, or as long as seven months at a time. At the end of the day, it wasn't ours to control. We saw it coming, but the ins and outs of regularity just do not exist in that world. In that regard, the norms of your household interactions and who does what are completely flexible. My wife had to be able to do everything. Then when I came home, I would want to do some things, which would mess up her process and get in the way.

My wife was the one who recommended that we look at the ROTC position, because then there would be a lot more stable environment transitioning forward away from the normal deployable military process. Basically, when I took this job at ROTC, all of a sudden my hours were for me to plan. It's very predictable in that manner. That actually did make the transition out of the Army easier.

My transitioning job with ROTC was at Dickinson College, a 2,600-student liberal arts college in Carlisle, Pennsylvania. It was definitely a different environment. I didn't have to deal with certain things before, or I could have just been a meathead if I wanted to. I had to figure out how to fit in there if I wanted to be successful, not only for myself but on behalf of my cadets. I had to soften the edges, I guess you'd say. That's the easiest way to say it. And I just figured it out.

I can't get out of bed in the morning and sit on the couch. It doesn't work for me. I have to do something or I get antsy.

With my background and my skill set, there have been plenty of offerings for full-time jobs. Generally, they are overseas for chunks of time and some of them are in combat zones. I'm not willing to do that. That's something we (my wife and I) decided before I stepped out of the service.

I really didn't have a whole lot of interest in going out and getting a job just to make money. Financially, we're in a spot where I don't have to. We're doing just fine with me sitting on my butt every day if that's what I choose to do. I think I've been driven by purpose for so long, and you could say the Army gave me a mission or a purpose.

We have a program where we teach law enforcement and first responders emergency trauma medicine. We got a grant through Blue Cross Blue Shield the last year when I was at Dickinson. I would basically teach the local law enforcement in the area. They call us up and we figure out a date and we pitch it to them.

I also work for a friend who has a contract with Barrett Firearms, who makes the huge, .50 caliber long-range rifles that the Navy SEALs use. We teach people how to employ their $12,000 toys that they've bought and don't know how to use—teaching them long-range shooting. Three days here, six days there.

I work for LABS and we do threat analysis and assessment for corporations. We do leadership decision-making classes. We do self-defense. We do risk mitigation. We teach CPR. We do all kinds of stuff for corporations.

I'm at a point now where I'm looking at a full-time job again. It's at a naval depot that is four miles from my house. I can run to work every morning. Basically, there are positions there that would more or less double my current income for working forty hours a week.

The military is pretty much all I knew my adult life. I graduated from high school in June of '90 and I was in the service by the end of July in '90. It's very structured. It's simple because they tell you what to wear and when to wear it and when to be where.

My wife and I made a decision a few years back that I wasn't going to try and be competitive for the next level of promotion. Basically, I had a pretty bad experience in Afghanistan with the loss of a teammate. I was the senior enlisted man on the team. You carry all of that with you.

There are practices in the Army that exist to help with this transition—theoretically. You've got to do the process and apply yourself and listen. It's just that the government is not always fast. If you stay by a military installation, those facilities and resources are available to you forever. You can go there and say, 'Hey, I need some help. Can you look at this resume for me? What do you think? This is the job I'm applying for.' and they will help you with those kinds of things.

Veterans need to be willing to look, ask questions, and seek help, because help is out there. It's not just within our community or in those programs. Most of the civilian community that I've come across has been nothing but helpful.

Most of what you do after a certain level in the Army has more to do with management and leadership. I think a good portion of the private sector knows that.

There's a smaller and smaller percentage of the population that are in the service. A generation ago, everybody knew somebody who'd served in World War II, Korea, or Vietnam, and everyone knew something about the military. When you look at right now, our population has less than 1 percent of the overall population who have served in the global war on terrorism. I think you're broadening the gap between the two environments, and that's the problem. We need to keep the two involved with each other to make sure everything works well.

I knew exactly how much I was going to make. If you retire from the Department of Defense, you basically go through a process by which the Veteran's Administration looks at how much damage you've acquired during your time in the service and provides disability payments above your base pay. We are very fine financially in all regards, even for the kid's college. That's not a concern. We have plenty of disposable income.

We saw it coming, so that's part of it. We managed a lot of it. I've also done some things throughout my career that enabled me to set myself up in that regard. I volunteered for some things that most people wouldn't, so I made more money throughout my career too. The other thing is, the wife and I have never really been running up debt.

7

RETHINKING RETIREMENT AFTER TEN YEARS: TIME FOR A RESET?

"Am I doing what I really want to do?"

Mary is reconsidering. She is at a point of asking herself which adjustments to make at this stage of her retirement.

describe this stage as 'unsettled' in the sense that I know my career—as I know it to be—is over. I would like to think that something else that I find in my retirement is going to engage me as much or be as fulfilling as my career was. I have found aspects of it in different things that I've gotten involved in, but I struggle with wanting to be involved in things but not wanting to be fully committed to a time schedule.

If I'm really interested in this, the time shouldn't be the issue, but I find it does become an issue with me. I don't like responding to deadlines anymore. I don't like having to be at certain meetings at certain times. That's the struggle to find meaning in your life as you get older.

I met my very good friend, who is close to the same age. Our thing right now is, am I doing what I really want to do? Am I doing something that really brings me joy or satisfaction, or does it make a difference? Why am I doing this? Does it make a difference? That's what I still struggle with sometimes. Does it make a difference, or do I really care? That conflict between yes, I care, but I don't want to put the time into it.

I don't want to feel like this when I become an eighty-five-year-old. That maybe I wasted these years—or could have used them better somehow. I think that goes back to the way you approach life. I don't want to say, 'I should have traveled to Africa. I should have done this. I should have done that.' I'm sitting here at seventy-eight and saying I don't know what those 'shoulds' are. Should there be any 'should' in my life? I'm just in a funny phase.

PART TWO

LIVING THE DREAM:
THE IDEAL LOCATION

S tart with your dreams. Where have you always wanted to live? Picking the ideal place to retire sounds easy. Your first reaction might be the place where you remember having the most fun. Then reality sets in, as you begin to bring a lot more variables into the equation. The location decision can't be made in a vacuum. Where you live has to fit with your goals for this stage of your life. Here are some questions raised by retirees that may be important in the decision:

- Who do I want to be near?
- What is the ideal climate? What are the risk factors for things like hurricanes, fires, earthquakes, or flooding?
- What can I afford?
- If I want to work part time, are the right opportunities available at this place?
- Can my hobbies be pursued in this location?
- Are there sufficient opportunities for intellectual stimulation?
- How is the access to health care?
- How does the community match up to my ideal? Have I read the local newspaper?
- What are the attractions in the region that are within easy driving distance?
- What would it be like to stay in my current location?

All of the people in this section had their own way of figuring out where to live. Their choices of location were remarkably different, but each fit their own set of priorities.

8

PIONEERING AS A SOLO FEMALE: THE RURAL COLORADO LIFESTYLE

"I like being out there at the edge. I like taking that risk."

Linda is in her mid-seventies and in good health. She lives alone in a rural area outside of Red Feather Lakes, Colorado. Her closest neighbors have four legs. She realizes that this is not the life for everyone and that there may come a day when health factors cause her to reconsider her location. When she and her ex-husband were looking for a place to live, they wanted to be close to nature and to have access to a community that was welcoming to newcomers. This community of 1,200 people met both criteria and gave them the unique lifestyle they were seeking.

Linda became involved with research about the community and became author of a series organized by the local historical society.

This stage of my life is very settled. Like many people in the second half of their seventies, I am starting to think about the future, given disabilities. Can I continue to live in a rural area where I'm sometimes snowed in? Am I too far away from services? Is it too long a drive to the hospital, blah blah blah. I would say these concerns are being addressed in an intellectual way. At the moment, I just enjoy every day and try to design my days in a way that maximizes my time outdoors and my time socializing with my friends.

My nearest neighbors are four-legged. Deer, the occasional moose, mountain lions, bobcats, and bears. Bears are pretty common. I like being out there at the edge. I like taking that risk. I live here alone. I feel totally safe. I hardly ever lock my door, even when I go into town. Only when I go for long periods of time do I lock the door. I have good neighbor support, but my neighbors aren't terribly close in proximity. There is a lot of community sharing and information flow, just marvelous support. I live in an area that's on a side of a mountain, so we have a pretty good slope. I don't bike or walk anywhere that doesn't go up or down at some point.

There are lots of old granite outcrops. One of the reasons that we were drawn to this area in the first place was that it looked remarkably like where we were living in Zimbabwe and Zambia, with the granite outcrops and large rock piles. They are great to climb, and great for lookout. We're surrounded by that kind of geography.

I like it. It suits me. I'll have been in this house for eighteen years this September. It was a spec house, so it was new when I first occupied it. Before that, I lived in a cabin in Red Feather Lakes. This is about a thousand feet lower in elevation than my cabin was. I'm not quite the pioneer woman that I was up there. I have a garage and a thermostat. I'm very grateful for those modern conveniences.

There are still some elements of pioneering. I definitely live according to the weather and the elements much more than people in urban areas do. Things bring us to a halt, and we just have to accept that.

In 2003, we had a storm that left us with five feet of new snow, and it was blowing. In some places, it had blown to eight feet. When I opened the garage door, the dog was in the garage with me and he looked up at this wall of snow as if to say, 'Well . . . whoa, how am I gonna get out?'

I was blocked in for about five days because of that particular storm. It was complicated by the fact that we got another eighteen inches on top of the five feet within another twenty-four hours. We had phone and we had electricity, unlike a lot of the state. I was writing for the newspaper at the time. I was close to deadline, but I was writing first-person features because I could telephone people and interview them and say, 'Well, what's it like in your neighborhood?'

For instance, I interviewed the owner of a large riding stable that was close by. He had to make sure a lot of horses were safe and fed. They were about a half-mile from his house. He had to slog through on snowshoes, and then he had to wrestle some hay free, and then he had to make sure the horses had enough. It was that real drama that I was trying to capture and pass on for the newspaper. I was pretty occupied.

The pros and cons of rural living come down to self-reliance. If it doesn't make you feel uncomfortable to be that far away from services—the degree to which you're distanced from those services—then come on in. I think you have to define what you mean by rural. Forty-five minutes is a fairly long drive. If something happened to my eyesight or I wasn't able to drive, I would not be able to live here. I think you have to feel fairly confident in your physical ability to do what you have to do.

One of the things that worries me about eventually moving into town is that I will, over time, be not as physically fit. Snow shoveling and walking for my mail are good exercise. The walk to my mail is about a mile round trip. Working on my plot is a lot of work. I do a lot of managing wildflowers and keeping weeds out. When you're outside as much as I've been, you become familiar with nature's signals. You listen to the birds. You know that if the magpies are all screaming, they're probably alerting the other birds to some dangerous situation. You look up and you think, 'Well what's there?' And right then— oh—it's a bobcat.

You get attuned to all the things around you. You know what's normal and you know what's not normal. In urban areas I think that's a lot harder to do, because there's just so much noise and light pollution. I hate light at night; I hate noise. We have the privilege of absolute silence here so often. When someone violates that, making excessive noise, they usually hear about it—not only from me. We don't really even have dogs barking because everybody so values the night skies and the silence.

You have to be happy, content enough in your own company to not feel the need to always have people around you. As I've been single for a long time, sometimes you can feel more lonely in an urban setting with a lot of people you don't know. In a rural setting you can be just listening, learning, taking in the weather, without feeling a need to be surrounded by people.

When we started looking around for places to live, we joked that we were like Hansel and Gretel out in a big forest. We had not lived in America very much. We hadn't traveled in America very much. We wanted to get off the Eastern Seaboard. We knew that we wanted high elevation and to have the opportunities for public land use.

One of the things that made Red Feather Lakes an ideal community was that it wouldn't take us fifty years to be accepted. One of the other places that we looked at felt like it would take us a lifetime to earn those folks' trust, to not appear suspicious to them. We have lots of people coming to Colorado from all different areas of the United States. Here, we felt we could just jump in and start doing, and that has definitely been the case. I just don't recall ever feeling like I wasn't part of the community.

I'm approximately forty-five minutes from Fort Collins, Colorado. I am probably about fifty-five minutes from Laramie, Wyoming. We look on the mountains, and we see the north-facing slopes of Rocky Mountain National Park. We're pretty isolated, except in the summer, when we have an influx of campers, hikers, Boy Scouts, Girl Scouts, et cetera—we tend to be a backwash. We're not at the park. We don't have a lot of services in Red Feather Lakes, which is my hub community village. I think in the last census, the town of Red Feather Lakes had a year-round population of about 1,200. That's way, way up in the summertime.

The summer community is a little different. They tend to know each other in different ways. They grew up with each other as kids. They now bring in their kids to the community. It's very much a hub in the summer, but in the wintertime, it gets pretty quiet.

There are communities within communities. My community has always centered around the excellent local library in Red Feather Lakes, where I volunteer. I have been on the board. My community and orbit are in that sphere and things that have radiated out from that. Politically, there's a Democratic Club which has created and fostered a lot of my friendships.

There is an intellectually stimulating group where you can listen to speakers and argue various points. That's been amazing for such a small community. We have a lot of retired academics because we're so close to Colorado State University. Some come from distant areas and land on our doorstep. To be able to harvest that knowledge is just a fabulous thing. We have speakers and we have programs, and it's very gratifying to me.

Then there are the other communities that have hubs around other common interests such as the bar. Those people that spend their time in the bar are people that I probably won't ever meet. They're there and their community is just as strong and just as viable, but it's not my community.

The historical society has quite a bit of money. They decided it would be useful for the community to have a virtual museum online. It's really an excellent website that people can go to. And they hired me to do oral histories with individuals about various aspects of the community. They more or less put me in charge. They made sure that I knew who they wanted me to interview to get a picture of this community from about the late fifties right through the current day. One of the oral histories was about the Forest Service. The national forest around us now is basically there for recreation and is filled with hiking trails and horseback riding trails—it's a destination. It's a playground here. It's almost as beautiful as Rocky Mountain National Park, but not nearly as important in peoples' minds.

In the 1950s, Red Feather had a huge wreath-making enterprise. A lot of the people who worked for the Forest Service started to make wreaths during the downtime from October to December. These were sent all over the United States. They would make as many as ten thousand Christmas wreaths. They even sent one to the White House.

Most of the people I interviewed were well known to me because I'd been a reporter doing feature stories for the local newspaper for fourteen years before I took on the historical society project. I interviewed these people when they still totally had good memories, and they could explain to me what happened. It was absolutely amazing. Two-thirds of those people have passed away since I interviewed them.

If someone hadn't interviewed them we would have lost all their insights, all their knowledge, all their history. Their oral histories keep them alive, in a way, and it has been a fabulous resource. We have the original interviews and photographs. Big notebooks full of these accounts are kept in the library, and we have made abbreviated versions that people can take home and read. It's all available online as well, and that's the virtual part of this museum.

9

LIFE IN A SENIOR CENTER: KEEPING A LOVE OF GARDENING

"I think that the continuing interest in plants kept me going."

> Paul has retired twice and is now continuing his passion for gardening while living in a senior center.

My background is teaching biology. I was a classroom teacher, and a counselor, and vice-principal, and principal, and superintendent of schools. I retired when I was fifty-six, so I retired early. Then I started a plant nursery in Los Gatos. I had that for a number of years and did landscape design work. I inherited a love of plants from my mother, I think.

As far as my background is concerned: as a Japanese American, I was in the internment camps during WWII, as part of the evacuation of Japanese Americans from the West Coast. We were put in a camp in Rohwer, Arkansas.

What the camp taught me was that isolating cultures was not the way to go. We could not isolate ourselves as something separate, as well. That if we'd be Americans, we'd need to be part of the culture. We strove to become leaders at the schools and student body presidents. We had decent grades and used our education to be successful.

I've been in the senior center for three years. The reason I picked this place for myself is the environment of the trees, and the grass, and the flowers, and the natural growth of the dry creek. This dry creek is a real treasure because they can't build around it—because it's so steep. And my apartment faces that dry creek. People are really lucky to live here.

I taught a course in horticulture in adult education after I retired. I gave a talk to the residents here as a guest speaker. That's been enjoyable. It's especially enjoyable if there are common interests. There are a lot of people who are interested in plants. They just don't have the background or the knowledge.

There is a section here at the senior center that is a flower garden for perennials. It's for all the residents to enjoy. It's more in the bluebell variety, and everything is geometric because of the hedges. A couple of the other residents have volunteered to help me in the garden, but some of them are older than I am, so it's difficult for them to do much work at all. I think they enjoy just being part of it and watching me work and being able to look at the plants.

I had been diagnosed with Parkinson's for over twenty years. As of late, I have not been able to walk well. It just came upon me suddenly. All that time, I knew I had Parkinson's, but it didn't affect me that much. Lately, it's been quite severe. I don't experience as much as I'd like now because I've been dependent on the crutches and canes. With Parkinson's, they say that it never gets better, it only gets worse, which is not encouraging. My mind is okay. I still have my senses with me. I just can't physically do the kind of work that I would like to do.

To dig a hole for plants, I have to have an escort with me all the time. It's not very productive. It's hard to communicate to people exactly what you should be doing. It's easier to do it yourself, even with a handicap.

I think that I would go crazy if it weren't for a hobby like plants. I think that my continuing interest in plants has kept me going through this. Without question, gardening satisfies my artistic interests. I can still remember my mother taking a walk and carrying a potato. When she saw a plant that she liked in the neighborhood, she cut it, then stuck the cutting in the potato to keep it alive and moist until she got home, and then she'd grow her own plant out of it.

10

THE RV LIFE: A GREAT WAY TO EXPLORE NORTH AMERICA

"We go down to the beach at sunset and blow the conch. You blow like you're blowing the trumpet. The other people on the beach are just staring at these crazy people."

Love of exploring. That's what fuels the RV lifestyle. Exploring mountains, national parks, and restaurants, all while sleeping in your own bed each night. When Andy and his wife retired in 2003, they realized their long-term dream by buying their first RV. The RV life evolved through three different stages for them, each with its own attractions. Their first RV adventures were short trips—they kept pretty close to home—but they'd usually make it to a location where they could enjoy hiking. Soon they moved on to their 'see North America' stage, visiting many of the great scenic wonders of the US, Canada, and Mexico. Their current stage is their 'snowbirding' stage, which has consisted of buying an RV lot in Florida and settling there for several months in the winter.

As far as my plans for retirement now, I don't have anything really long term. It's been about 'going with the flow.' It's been going from the grandkids' soccer to baseball and babysitting. I think it's very grandkids-centric right now. Between that and RV-ing and just going with the flow. I don't have any lofty goal that I'm shooting for at this point other than to keep living.

We take the grandkids camping in the RV. That's always fun. We keep them from fighting. They have bunks in the RV. They look forward to it. We do it once a year with them. That's about all we can manage.

When we first got the RV, we would take trips with destinations that were largely areas where we could hike, like West Virginia. It was all fairly close-by stuff. Then we just expanded from there. We just always felt that there is so much to see in North America. I'll say North America instead of just in the USA. You can go a lifetime driving around and seeing new things. Our national park system is absolutely phenomenal. We don't think there's a lot that we haven't seen. We were more into the nature sites, the Yosemites and those places.

I enjoy researching in advance and planning out and saying, 'Well, what's in this area? What do we have to see? What are we going to do?' That's the part that I like the most.

We typically take a trip in January, February, March. We go to Florida a lot. Last year, we did a Western trip, and we've made two or three Western trips. All in all, I think we've seen probably 90 percent of the national parks that are west of the Mississippi, and also up into Canada. There's been a lot of fun.

There are tons of national parks that we like. We love Sequoia. We liked all the ones in Nevada, and Zion and Arches, and I forget what the other one is. We like all the mountainous types of parks. But we've also been to some that are more desert-oriented in Arizona.

The one that surprised me the most was Death Valley. We got a campground and I was just thinking it's another national park. We'd get to tick that off. We really didn't expect much. It was really pretty amazing. It's a monstrous park and it's got everything from just raw desert to mountains and lakes. There's an Air Force base near there, and they literally practice flying through canyons in Death Valley with the fighter jets.

We've done one RV caravan. We did this last summer with an organization called Fantasy RV Tours. It was an eight-day tour into Mexico and we actually had twenty-nine RVs going across the border into Mexico. The interesting thing was, we didn't even have to stop when we crossed into Mexico. They just waved us right through. All twenty-nine, just like a freight train. They had this one guy who is sort of a local. He was American, but he lived in Mexico. He was a facilitator who made all the arrangements. They wind up donating to some sort of a fund. I don't know if that's the 'police chief's back pocket fund' or if it's truly some other thing. They had the cops out on all the intersections blocking traffic so our twenty-nine RVs could roll away through town. That was kind of funny.

Last year we did a 6,600-mile trip. That's a lot of driving. We're both getting tired of sitting on our butts all day long driving. We've done a number of those trips, into Mexico, Canada, Jasper, and Banff.

My favorite destination is actually Siesta Key in Florida. It's a little county campground. As you turn into the campground, you're headed straight for the Gulf of Mexico. It's only a long city block to the Gulf of Mexico. There are forty campsites, twenty on either side of that road, and they're right there on the beach. We love that place.

This sounds crazy, but our little cadre hangs out together at sunset facing west. At sunset, we usually take a glass of wine or a cocktail in our hands and we go down to the beach to watch the sun go down under the waves. What you do at sunset is you blow the conch. I think it started in Key West. I got a conch with the end cut off. You blow like you're blowing the trumpet. We have a lineup of about six guys and gals, and you're standing there. The other people on the beach are just staring at these crazy people.

After having taken long trips for a number of years, now we're more in a snowbird mode. We want someplace where it's warm in the wintertime.

When you're traveling—even with that caravan—it's not as social. You do meet people on the way, but you only see them for three or four days. It's not like you're going to have lasting friendships. Only if you start staying places for weeks at a time, otherwise I don't think that friendship occurs.

Campgrounds get sold in a hurry. For me, to get a campground in Florida, I have to start a year in advance. There's been such a growth in the number of RVs. The campgrounds just have not kept up. We said, 'Well, let's find a place to *buy*; then we don't have to worry about getting in.' I'd been researching on the internet. We wanted to be reasonably close to beaches. We wanted to be not too far from a city. I'd look and see something, and then I'd pull it up on Google Maps.

When we got to Crystal River, we just looked at each other and said, 'Yes, this is the one.' They've got swimming pools. They've got an exercise room with treadmills. Pretty social environment. There's a bunch of people there from Michigan and quite a few people from Ohio too. I'm sure we will get into the swing of things when we get down there, once the other snowbirds arrive.

We'll leave the RV through the summer. You're supposed to leave the air conditioning at around eighty-five. You don't want the RV cooking through the summer, so most people just set the air conditioner up real high. You get a couple of desiccant buckets to absorb moisture.

I'd never driven an RV in my life. The owner did take me on a little test drive that lasted maybe fifteen minutes with me driving. They're big and it's pretty scary when you first start out. You just try to get a feel for how close you are to the side of the road, and how close to the middle. You sort of assume that the centerline gives you enough room to the right to clear. What you wind up doing is you watch your mirrors on the left side and you see where the centerline is sitting while you're going down the road.

One interesting episode was when we took this trip to do some hiking over toward Pennsylvania. At that time, I had a GPS that was a regular car kind of a GPS. We were going from one campground to another on a two-lane road down a steep hill, and at the bottom of the hill was a stoplight. The GPS told me to turn left at the stoplight. I got to the intersection. I turned left, and I was like, 'Whoa, it's a covered bridge and we definitely don't fit under that covered bridge.' I'm stuck in the middle of this intersection with this RV and towing a car behind us. When you tow a car with one of these RVs, you cannot back up. I was just in the middle of the intersection, trying to disconnect. In the meantime, a good Samaritan was out there directing traffic around us. We had to back up and go down the road, and there was a bridge that didn't have a roof on it that we could go across the river on.

You have to have a pretty good DIY mentality. There are lots of little things that wind up going wrong with RVs. You take your house and drag it down the road bouncing around, and you can imagine that things come loose, things break. Yes, there's lots of stuff like that, and I enjoy that.

I once suggested to my wife that we should get rid of the sticks and bricks and just go full-time RV. She wasn't having any part of that.

11

BALANCING CULTURE AND FAMILY: INFLUENCES ON RETIREMENT LOCATION

*"I've always had a quest, a burning desire
to find a place that feels like home."*

Pedro is a Cuban immigrant contemplating the elements of
his retirement. He and his wife are examining the trade-offs
of various locations.

A concern that I have is, where do I want to live after I end
working here? We really love Alabama. It's a beautiful state,
a culture of civility. It's opening up to the rest of the world,
plenty to do, low taxes, low regulations, but we have no family here.
It's not *home* home; because of the fact that I am a Cuban exile, I
associate more with Southeast Florida.

I've always had a quest, a burning desire to find a place that feels
like home. I have come to realize that I will always be a stranger in a
strange land. I've also realized that that is probably a common human
condition. I think that we will perhaps end up where one of our two
daughters are. That would be my goal as a Cuban, to hopefully end
somewhere near my immediate family. That's what my wife and I

long for. She too is an immigrant. She's from Colombia, and that's what we'd love.

Southeast Florida is no longer what it was. I mean, it's a ton of people. A lot of issues that go with high density, but it calls to me probably more than anywhere else that we've lived.

I don't know if other immigrants feel the same way or not, but they probably do. The way that they tend to gravitate toward each other—like in Miami, it's Cubans. It's the same with the Mexicans in Chicago, Houston, Dallas, LA. Maybe that's what I should do. Man, I love to get a cup of Cuban coffee, but after two, I may have had enough.

12

LIVIN' ON TULSA TIME: ADAPTING TO A NEW COMMUNITY

"Moving to Tulsa was starting all over together, building friendships and deciding what was there available to share together."

Jan is in her early seventies and retired fifteen years ago as dean of a medical school in Chicago. Upon retirement, she reminded her husband, Jack, of his promise that they could retire close to Jan's parents in Oklahoma. There are those who believe that Jack's agreeing to this should have resulted in his being named "Husband of the Year."

Together they faced the challenges of adapting to a new community. Jan is an outgoing and gregarious person, and Jack is easygoing and friendly. Building a network of new friends came naturally to them. Participating in community activities and volunteering were important elements of their integration into the community.

About fifteen years ago, my husband Jack and I decided that it was time to retire and that we wanted to experience different things during our retirement. Our kids had gone different directions. We didn't know where they would end up, so we couldn't really follow the kids. We made that decision.

Jack had always promised me that after we worked and raised our family, he'd take me back to my home state of Oklahoma to be near my parents and family. We have vacationed in Tulsa a lot, so it was comfortable. It felt like a place that was affordable. It was recommended for retirees and was not that far from our Chicago friends. It was not that far from our kids, who were in Denver and Austin. They could come through Tulsa pretty easily. Those were the main reasons that we went there.

We had gone to Tulsa a number of times to look for housing. We'd already purchased a house. My brother and sister-in-law had great recommendations for doctors, hospitals, dentists, any type of thing. That made it easier to fit into the community.

But it was more difficult for Jack because it wasn't his family. Although he was really welcomed warmly, he didn't feel like he'd finished work. Fortunately, his company offered him a consulting job, which he did for about three years.

When we said we were moving to Tulsa, everyone said, 'Why would you go to Tulsa?' It was not something that people had heard about very often. Jack and I knew that it had things that we would really like: better weather, warmer winters, cultural things like symphonies, opera, and one of the top ballet companies in the world. We do enjoy them on a regular basis. The climate allows us longer golf, biking, and hiking seasons. We love to do all those things.

The other thing that's been really enjoyable for us was the family time with my parents, my brother and sister-in-law, and some extended family. It's convenient during the holidays and an obviously great place to root for my alma mater, the Oklahoma Sooners. What could be more fun than watching a nationally ranked football team? These are comfortable and enjoyable things.

It's hard to leave a big city like Chicago, where you get first-run theater productions and you have the concerts and professional sports and so much. Yes, it felt a little like we stepped down a level in Tulsa, because we thoroughly enjoyed what was available to us in Chicago.

Moving to Tulsa was starting all over together, building new friendships and exploring what the city had to offer. It was a trade-off. We gave up things in Chicago, but we really don't miss the traffic or those long cold winters. I think if you're someone who looks for the positive, you focus on those things when you're in a new place. The theater was easy to get to. It met our needs. We may not have the Chicago Symphony Orchestra, but there are some great symphonies here. It's turned out really well.

When we moved to Oklahoma, I was referred to an optometrist. She knew some of my family, so she asked me questions about how long we had been here and how we liked Tulsa. I said, 'I miss my friends, I really miss my friends.' After the eye exam, she said, 'I have a client I think you'd really enjoy. Do you mind if I give her your phone number?' I like to say that the rest is history. We clicked. She and her husband are two of our dearest friends in Tulsa. She invited me to join her book club. Through the book club, we met friends from all over Tulsa who have parties and events. We met a couple who invited us to play golf with them, and another couple invited us to join their church. All because one person took the time to make a phone call and make that connection.

Another wonderful thing about Tulsa is that it's a giving city with lots of opportunities for us to volunteer.

The newest thing to Tulsa is a park called the Gathering Place. There's a local philanthropist by the name of George Kaiser. He's a remarkable person who had a vision to build a park along the riverfront of the Arkansas River. The mission of the park was to provide a place for everyone. The park is different. It's not like Disney World, where the tickets to get in are expensive. The Gathering Place is free. That's what is so amazing. It opened September the 8th of 2018. Jack and I became volunteers a month later. We do guest services. We're at the welcoming center, which is called the Williams Lodge. We love to hand out maps and welcome visitors to the Gathering Place.

One day a father and son came in together. The little boy said, 'Daddy, you finally brought me to the park. I'm so excited we're here.' I said, 'Are you going to ride the boats today?' The boy said, 'Daddy, can we ride the boats?' The man looked at me and he said, 'No, we probably have to pay to ride on the paddleboats or take the canoes or the kayaks out.' I said, 'Nope, they're all free!' On their way out, the little boy came up to tell me what a great day he had had and that he got to ride on one of the boats.

I graduated to the next level of docent. I tell everyone I got my master's degree in the Gathering Place. I had to beg and plead my way in. That was an additional two months of training once a week.

The park was built for sustainability. The trees that they had to cut down they've turned into benches that you can sit on. They planted 1.2 million plants and shrubs in the park and 5,789 trees. You can't reserve any seating area. It's first come, first served. They have movie nights for families to bring their kids to see a movie and sit on the Great Lawn that seats about 5,000 people. That's all free. They have concerts. The Roots from *The Tonight Show* were the band who played at the park's Grand Opening.

I go home from the park feeling so excited. It's meant a lot for Jack and me personally to be a part of this and see what it has brought to the city. It's a place that is designed to educate, excite, and engage.

There are no rides that you get on. You go over hills and around curves and up in the air. It's all kid power. The kids have to climb rope ladders. They go across rope bridges from tower to tower. They go on swings. You can see downtown Tulsa and the Arkansas River. It's pretty spectacular.

13

DOWNSIZING THE FARM: THE NEXT ADVENTURE

"We'd like to go to the Virginia farm adventure next."

Ellen and John use geographic moves to add a sense of adventure to their lives. Each move has been more than just a change of location. It gives them a new vitality, new activities, and new friends. They decide together what will be their next adventure.

John had wanted to work in a small village in Alaska, so they did that for a couple of years. Then they moved to a seventy-five-acre farm in Pennsylvania, and soon added the challenge of raising Icelandic sheep. As they entered their seventies, after sixteen years on the farm, they realized that physically managing the sheep was becoming tough on the bones. It was also a time when they wanted to be closer to family. They are in the midst of their next adventure of moving to a three-acre farm in Virginia and learning to board horses, while playing a bigger role in the kids' and grandkids' lives.

Ellen: For sixteen years we've had a seventy-five-acre farm in Northeastern Pennsylvania, where we are now. We're in the process of selling it next year and moving down to Virginia. That's going to be a big change for us again. We want to be closer to our sons who live in Virginia.

John: We've got a nice farm, with buildings and pastures. We wanted to try and make some money from the farm also. I was still employed full time. We had chickens and ducks and we're selling eggs and things like that.

Some friends in New York State had Icelandic sheep. They were saying they'd sell us some Icelandic sheep.

Ellen: They were rare in this country then. The wool is very heavy wool. It's like two layers and is something you would wear in very cold weather.

John: We were able to milk them and make cheeses, sell them for meat, or sell their wool. They were larger than some of the other breeds.

Ellen: We decided that, knowing nothing about sheep, we were going to do this. Farming while still working was an attempt to make a little money with it. That turned out to be a joke.

John: The sheep really are characters. They're all individuals. They're interesting characters that really do have individual personalities. We had one who was our main girl. Her name was Hwind. She was a great mom. She had a nice way of taking care of all the rest.

Ellen: They're pretty smart.

John: We would breed them. We would buy new rams and sell some of our rams for meat and keep increasing the flock. At our highest point, we were at almost one hundred sheep.

Ellen: It was a bit much.

John: I was still working full time. All the care and attention—which we hadn't really thought about—got to be a little too hard.

Ellen: They're very strong. There was a lot of wrestling and getting dragged around the ground a lot. Yes, reality hit us, I guess. We still enjoy them though. They were so wonderful, the little rams bouncing up and down in our fields.

John: Because I had surgery on my back three years ago, I just can't wrestle them anymore. If you pick them up they'll wrestle you back, I'm telling you.

Ellen: Actually, one hit my knee and destroyed my knee. I had to get a new knee. You've got to be physically fit to do it.

John: People think they're just little sheep. I was trying to work a deal out with the local high school football team and bring the guys up to try to tackle them. They'd have a hell of a time trying to catch them and would really improve their football skills.

Ellen: The grandkids loved it up here because we live on top of a mountain, and so you have lots of forest and then lots of field. It's been great for them. It's been a little painful thinking we're going to sell the farm.

With the chickens and the ducks we have, the grandkids come and they get the eggs with us and help to feed them. We're going to bring our chickens and ducks with us when we move south.

I'm going to be seventy and he'll be seventy-one in January. There's a lot of care that needs to be put in to seventy-five acres to make it look decent. We live in a very old farmhouse that we have spent years fixing up. It's always needing a lot of upkeep. Things are getting harder up here.

Here in Pennsylvania, I volunteer for a little theater cultural center every Tuesday all day with the same group of people. It just makes me feel good to be helping somebody. It's all nonprofit. It's still a little dinky thing, but what I do is make these gifting packages for people to buy, which makes money for the organization. It is a fun thing and I enjoy the people very much. John is cooking at the soup kitchen. He has fun with these old men.

John: There's these ministerial guys and me. One of our priests, he's only Christian on Sunday. He's older. He's retired too.

Ellen: They have fun working together. They laugh and joke and they make tons of food. They feed sixty or seventy people a night and they do it two or three times a month.

John: I can't get over the amount of food we prepare, right? We always have two main courses, a starch, two vegetables, and soup and salad and dessert.

Ellen: The regulars are the characters in the town you would see walking up and down the street. There's these two ladies who come an hour and a half early and they sit out front. They kind of flirt with our retired priest. I'm trying not to be rude about how they look, but they wear skintight tank tops with no bra on and they weigh about 250.

John: Our grandson Drew is seven and he came to the soup kitchen with me one time. We got to dude it up with his apron and a little bowl-like hat to wear. They were having chicken tenders that I always called Drew's chicken. Everybody was saying, 'Can I have some more of that chicken?' I'd say 'Drew's chicken?' He would just smile.

Ellen: He was so cute. We put an apron on him that was tons too big for this little fellow. He's working with all these old men and they were all so great to him. Showing him how to make fifty pounds of potatoes and he was just blown away by it all.

John: The Virginia farm is only three acres. It's easier to take care of. It's got three horse stalls and potential for a fourth one. A lot of people have been telling us to think about trying to board some horses. We'd like to go to that adventure next.

Ellen: That's another learning curve for us. It wouldn't be more than three horses. Just board them. People would come and care for them themselves most of the time.

We're still in the country and the house sits back down a long driveway. It's like a smaller version of where we are now. It's a smaller house, a little newer house, a lot less acreage, but John's still going to be doing what he likes to do. The older I get, the more I want to be closer to our two sons and two grandkids. I want to be there for when they go do class things and have concerts. I never used to get to do that. We kept thinking we want to be down closer to them.

John: Following through with some of their stuff. Like, one of our granddaughters was in this concert and we're four and a half hours away. We just don't get down there to that kind of stuff.

Ellen: The thought of having horses boarding there would just tickle her to death. I just want to have a chance to have her for a full day at a time and bring her home or overnight and do it much more often than three or four times a year. I hope that will work out with the kids.

This past spring, our youngest son went driving around with us. We saw a house we all liked and our youngest son spent the next three months convincing us that we had to move down this year or next year. We're doing it.

Our kids participated in the process, the youngest son especially. He's gone through the whole process. I flipped out when we saw it, and told him, 'Yes, we liked this one house.' Then I was scared to death to do it.

The youngest son has done everything to get it, just to make sure we're there. He wants us down there so bad. That's neat to know—that he wants us that much. On the other hand, I wonder if I got talked into this and worry we won't like it for some reason.

My sister has lived in the attached part of our current house for the last ten years. She's not coming down to Virginia. We're really close, so selling this place is going to be very painful for me and her. We're going to put this house up for sale in March. That's when the real estate says it's a good time to start. We didn't put it up sooner because I was giving my sister this whole year to move. We don't know how long it'll take for this house to sell with the seventy-five-acre property. We still need a decent amount for it. We can't sell it for nothing.

John: Our biggest concern, overwhelmingly, is selling the house here.

Ellen: That's for *you*. Moving away from my sister is very painful for me. The other thing is, am I going to meet people down there? That's probably why I want to volunteer or do something like that to meet people. Scared of being lonely, I guess. I'm turning seventy in February and then this move. I hope it's going to be good, because I'm still a little nervous. I'm ready to go, but I'm nervous. This will hopefully be the last major move for us, which in a way is a little scary. Then, knowing us, we will probably move again! I don't know.

14

INDEPENDENT LIVING AT AGE 102: MAINTAINING AN ACTIVE LIFESTYLE

"Sometimes independent living has some challenges."

> **Dorothy is enjoying her independent living at a facility in Memphis. She has a routine of activities that provides social connections to the others at this location.**

'm very relaxed. Yes, and I'm comfortable. I'm happy. This is a facility for people for independent living. Lutheran Village is very comfortable. The people are friendly and everyone seems to get along really well. I've heard of different places where the residents don't always get along really well, and that wouldn't be much fun. I've been here over thirteen years.

My apartment is small. I do have a balcony, and I have a lot of potted plants on the balcony that I take care of. That keeps me busy and I enjoy having the blooming flowers out there. I'm on the second floor. When I'm just sitting in my living room I look out at my distant trees, and I love trees.

I play canasta twice a week on Tuesday and Friday night. I've been playing canasta for at least sixty years. Canasta is an easy game to play. Of course you have to think some about what you're doing, but mostly you're visiting with the people that you're playing with, and I enjoy that. The main thing I get out of the card games is the fellowship with the other players. The canasta is the excuse for getting together, I guess you can say.

I do sit at the front desk. We have a front desk here that people come to from the outside to see people here. Someone at the front desk has to answer the phone and greet the people that come in. A lot of people don't want to do it, but I enjoy meeting the people who come in.

Sometimes independent living has some challenges. I'm getting to the place where I can't do a lot of things or I'm too old. I was in a car wreck about six years ago. A man ran a red light and hit me, so it stopped me from driving. People had been trying to get me to quit driving anyway, but I didn't really drive much. I went to church and church-related things and just went to the grocery store, but it was best for me to quit driving. I really miss my driving very, *very* much. All my life I've had a car at my disposal and to *not* have a car really is hard. It's very hard.

We have a birthday party once a month for all the residents who've had a birthday that month. Everyone who lives here is invited to the birthday party. I enjoy sending birthday cards to a lot of people here in the building and some who don't live here. I enjoy *getting* cards, so in order to get cards, you know, you have to send a few.

Then they have a bus that carries us different places. On Tuesdays the bus carries us to the grocery store or the post office or the bank. Then about once a month they'll have a day trip to a casino or other various places. On Thursdays they usually take us shopping in different places every month. I go to church every Sunday.

I love to cook, but I don't cook much anymore because it's just me I'm cooking for. I love to cook when somebody is going to be here. I made a pot of vegetable beef stew on the stove. I love to bake. I make a cheese wafer that my family enjoys so much. I bake cookies.

We have to be fifty-five or older to live here. There are two or three people just over the fifty-five-year limit, but most of them are in their eighties and nineties. Over my thirteen years at Lutheran Village, a lot of people have moved in and out for various reasons. Some have passed away and some have had to go to nursing homes or to move in with their families, so there are various reasons for leaving here. I don't think anyone has ever left Lutheran Village because they didn't like it. This is a very pleasant place to live. The residents get along and are happy together.

15

CULINARY AND LITERARY EXPLORING: THE BEST OF THE CAROLINAS

"We just love taking day trips, following a lot of the chefs who are growing in popularity in the Carolinas."

Joe and his wife retired ten years ago and decided to move to the Carolinas to be closer to family and their roots. They live in the small town of Flat Rock, North Carolina.

Retirement allows someone the time to pursue lifelong passions. One of their passions is being foodies and appreciating innovative cooking. One of their unexpected delights in the Carolinas has been exploring and discovering the number of award-winning chefs who work within a few hours' drive of their home.

Their second passion is literary. On those same restaurant day trips, they visit local bookstores, as well as the homes of authors and the settings for their work.

Time and place intersect perfectly so they can immerse themselves in their passions. Their location in the Carolinas gives them access; their retirement schedule gives them the time.

've been retired for probably a little over ten years now, with the first three of those years being on the West Coast. We finally decided to move back to our roots, the Southeast. It's where our family is. We ended up doing that in 2013. We're real happy that we're back here in the Southeast—away from those high costs of the West Coast. I guess we're two of those many baby boomers who have left the state of California.

We're in a little village called Flat Rock. It's about thirty miles south of Asheville. The town of Greenville, South Carolina is just south of us by about thirty miles. We're in between two larger towns. What we're enjoying here in Flat Rock is the proximity to lots of interesting towns.

At this point in time, we love our travel. We just love taking trips. What I mean by that is day trips. Where we are in Carolina, that affords us the opportunity to get in the car and drive three hours and just have lunch at one of our favorite little places.

Having been on a plane almost my entire career, I just love now the flexibility; we don't have to worry about the reservations. We're just extremely flexible in that respect. We like to go by ourselves, which allows us to build our own schedules. Many times our decision to travel occurs that morning, because we really haven't thought that far ahead.

These towns were agrarian. They lived and died by the tobacco industry. These towns were just folding up. These restaurants and these chefs have come in and they've become a destination for a lot of people. You're talking, in some cases, *busloads* of people showing up on excursions just to go to these restaurants for lunch or for dinner. It's been really quite interesting. It's been a whole new spin.

It really provides us that opportunity to get around to these different older places. They are almost like the town of Mayberry in the old Andy Griffith TV show. We enjoy that culture, that hometown feeling, and we're really enjoying exploring new restaurants and finding new chefs we'd like to follow. We love following a lot of the chefs that are really growing in popularity in this part of the country. Many of them are James Beard Award nominees.

When it comes to finding restaurants, that's where I hand it over to my wife. She is a great chef, a cookbook chef. She will sit down and read a cookbook like I will sit down and read *The Prince of Tides* by Conroy. She loves reading cookbooks.

There's a magazine that's unique here to the Southeast. It's called *Garden & Gun*. It covers the culinary scene in the Southeast. It discusses the up-and-coming chefs, those who receive James Beard nominations and so on. We then try to track them down. We'll say, 'Hey, let's plan a trip there. Let's plan a trip here.' That's my wife's doing for the most part. I'm the willing participant. I get in the car and drive us to these places. We may spend one night or two nights or it'll be just a day trip.

We love traveling to the coast, whether it be to Savannah or Charleston. We like running to Oxford, Mississippi, which is an overnight trip. That's the home of Faulkner, the University of Mississippi, and great restaurants. John Currence is an owner-chef and has a great little restaurant that we've been to called City Grocery.

For one of our trips, we said, 'Let's go to Chapel Hill.' We had two nights of reservations at these James Beard award-winning chefs' restaurants. During the day, we just would walk around the beautiful campus of the University of North Carolina. We walked into a bar and happened to sit down right next to the mayor. He said, 'I overhead you were going to this restaurant, that restaurant, but failed to mention the best restaurant I think we have here in town. That's Merritt's Grill. Best BLT you'll ever have. It's toasted sourdough bread. You can get a single, a double, or a triple, with tomatoes and lettuce. It's magnificent.'

It's an old renovated gas station, and they've just put gravel out front and tables with umbrellas. You walk in and you just say, I'll take a single, a double, or a triple. That's all they do, BLTs. We actually had driven there just for the day on our anniversary because that's what we wanted—a BLT for lunch.

The Southeast cooking is getting quite a bit of notice. There's one place that's in Kinston, North Carolina, and it's been on the PBS program called *A Chef's Life*. It's all about Vivian, who used to cook in New York City and work for all these top chefs. She wanted to open a restaurant. Her parents said they'd love to help her if she'd open her restaurant back home in Kinston. Let me tell you, this restaurant is really good. It's one of those farm-to-table type of restaurants. It's all about knowing who is producing your food, and understanding the butchering process of the meats. She really does a good job.

We enjoy being able to get to these smaller towns. We're kind of book nuts as well. When we go to these little towns, we're always looking for these older, antiquated bookstores. I collect a lot of fly fishing books. Many of them come from Scotland or Wales or England. Believe it or not, these bookstores have some real gems.

The Southeast is a great literary hub. Lots of great authors have their roots in the Southeast. John Grisham now calls Chapel Hill home part of the time. We live right next door to Carl Sandburg's place where he wrote. In about fifteen minutes, I can hike to a spot where he used to sit down on a rock outcropping and do a lot of his writing.

Having moved back here is the reason I've picked up Pat Conroy. I have devoured everything he has written. He has become one of my favorite writers. He wrote about so many different things and places. Pat graduated from The Citadel and played basketball there. One of my favorite Conroy books is *My Losing Season*. I can really identify with that in all ways because of the sports I played back in those days.

We were at a bookstore in Columbia, South Carolina, talking to the owner after buying a Conroy book. He said, 'Pat used to come in here all the time.' One day, one of his employees came running up to him and said, 'Jim, Jim, you've got to come out front. There's some guy just writing in all the books.' It was Pat Conroy, just signing his books that were sitting on the shelf to be sold. He said Pat was quite the character.

I do like some Civil War books. One of my favorites is *The Killer Angels* by Michael Shaara. To talk about that here in the South is sacrilege. They call it the 'Yankee Aggression' here in the South instead of the Civil War. I look for a first edition of that. It really opened my eyes to the Civil War. I just thought it was an outstanding book in the way it was written.

The literary scene is strong in part because of the colleges and universities that are so prevalent around here and so important to the Carolinas. Within a circumference of twenty miles you've got the University of North Carolina, you have Duke, you have North Carolina State, and then not far off is Wake Forest. You've got the University of South Carolina in Columbia.

I think a lot of the bookstores that we tend to go to are located in university towns. They're smaller towns, and the Barnes and Nobles really didn't make it to them. I just think the universities and the students really kept the small bookstores alive. We just love going into these musty old places. You can just smell the history. It's amazing.

We try to tie the two together—the literary and culinary. If there's a restaurant we'd like to go to, we'll make a reservation, then look to see if there are any bookstores nearby.

We're always looking for an up-and-coming chef who is just beginning to get notoriety or a chef who owns their restaurant. It's the geography that allows that to happen. It's been fun, it's really been fun.

16

RETURNING TO YOUR ROOTS: A LONG-TERM EXPAT COMES HOME

"I'm suddenly back in touch with my old school."

> After spending his working life overseas, Clark and his wife have returned to his hometown of Virginia Beach, where they have reconnected with the community.

did not really have a voice in the matter of timing my retirement. It's what they call a RIF, or 'reduction in force.' This HR guy said to me, 'Why are you still working?' I said, 'Well, I really like what I do. It's just a fun job. I'm living in a neat place and all that stuff.' He said, 'Well, you have already maxed out your retirement benefits. You're not going to get any more. You can leave right away with maximum benefits.' Then I understood that they wanted me to do that.

The retirement sort of came upon me in a surprising way. I had not given any thought to what I wanted to do or where I was going to live. I immediately started thinking about what some of my options might be. I was very fortunate that my parents had just moved out of their family home into a retirement home. I had purchased it from them as a rental property. I just looked at the lease agreement, and

I noticed that the lease was up for renewal, and right about the time that I would be leaving my job.

My wife and I talked about it, and we thought, 'Well, let's just go back to Virginia. We'll park ourselves in this home until we can figure out what we're going to do.' We had a place to go to.

People I went to high school with, people I went to college with, and my parents were all here. Virginia Beach has always been for me a very pleasant place to live. It has some of the best climate in the world—not too hot in the summer, not too cold in the winter. This would be the place to live.

I went to an alumni luncheon for Norfolk Academy, which I had attended more than forty years ago. The headmaster of the school happened to have been my history teacher back in 1957. He had not seen me since then, but he had kept up with me. He approached me about a fundraising position. He needed someone to contact and encourage alumni to put the school in their will, to take out a charitable trust, to be good to the school, things like that. After first turning him down, I then realized that I was probably going to need something to do. Did I want to volunteer? Did I want to do this? Did I want to do that? When he came back the second time and said, 'Look, we really want you to take this job, so please sign the contract and return it to me and start work in August,' I talked it over at length with my wife and I said, 'Well, why not? What do we have to lose?'

So I accepted and went to work as the Director of Planned Giving. It was a perfect activity for me. I'm suddenly back in touch with my old school, which meant I was back in touch with my classmates. It was an immediate reentry into a very wide social network.

I really enjoy having more time with my wife. I'm always interested in learning more about what she's been through, and the Middle East. In little old Virginia Beach, we have discovered a whole new community of friends who went to the American University of

Beirut and the American University in Cairo. They are sometimes third and fourth generation Lebanese immigrants who've come over here. Their families came over here eighty or ninety years or so ago. Most of them are Lebanese-Americans now. Some of them don't even speak Arabic, because they were born here, and they have lived here all their lives, and some of them have immigrated recently. My wife and I are enjoying being socially active in two completely different communities.

As I'm turning seventy-eight, what's been a little upsetting is seeing people of that age who are suddenly here one day and gone the next. I never really experienced that overseas, because when we were working overseas, we were all kind of in the same age group. It was very rare to suddenly lose a friend. Here, you settle down and you work into these various groups and you start seeing people frequently. Then suddenly one of them dies, and you go to the church.

PART THREE

CHOOSING TO WORK: REWARDS OF NEW KINDS OF WORK

The next three sections of the book have stories about activities that people undertake in their retirement. This first section is stories about different kinds of work that fits their new lifestyle. The following two sections have stories about leisure activities and volunteering. Those three sets of activities add up to a significant amount of baby boomer potential to reinvent themselves.

There's a transition that several of our interviewees have talked about. During your working years, the alarm clock went off. You were compelled to get up and be at work on time. You were given assignments. You had deadlines. You had to comply so you could pay the rent. It was full time. That's work. The job was a major focus and often a source of your personal identity.

For forty-plus years, you may have been focused on a job, having a routine, a clear set of activities, and direction from your boss. Those boundaries and behaviors may have had a lasting impact on you. It may be time for some unlearning. As you will hear from some of the interviewees, something may feel weird and unnatural about no longer having a primary focus.

'Unfocus,' if you want. It's okay. Several of the people you will meet in the next sections have a bit of this and a bit of that. Maybe a bit of gig work, some volunteering, or a new hobby. Each day is different. Each day is a new adventure. And it's nice to be in charge of how much or how little of each of these activities feels right to you.

Multiple activities are different and take some getting used to. For some, it may take a different way of organizing yourself and your calendar. For others, it may take a new attitude of less planning and taking life as it comes. Once you have your new routines, it can be rewarding in a way that is unlike anything you saw during your full-time employment.

This section talks about people who continue to work. Why would they want to work, after all of those years pursuing a career? The answers may not be simple, but they'll likely blend some of the following factors raised by retirees:

- Additional money to maintain one's lifestyle
- Camaraderie with fellow workers or customers
- A sense of purpose
- Opportunity to try something never done before
- Filling available time

Your best path forward may be to continue in your present job, or modify it for this next stage of your life. Fewer hours or different responsibilities could be a fit for both you and your employer. Or you may build on your current skills, but apply those skills in remarkable new directions. You may work every bit as hard as when you had a 'job,' but the difference is that your new driver is the joy of the work, rather than the dictates of a boss. In several of the following cases, the interviewees are willing to test their limits and try something new.

17

REINVENTING NOT ONCE BUT TWICE: A LONG WAY FROM BEING A DIPLOMAT

"I had to reinvent myself and I'm so glad I was able to do that because that just opened up a whole new area for me to develop myself in."

Chuck retired as a diplomat in the Foreign Service at age fifty. He wanted to get something different out of the next stage of his life. He embraced change and set out on his new path.

Reinvention number one was to start a for-profit birdwatching tour company that focused on Africa. Birdwatching is a long way from being a career diplomat, but he knew Africa, he had a passion for birdwatching, and he had developed managerial skills. He boldly embarked on this new path.

Reinvention number two was to be a founder of a nonprofit wilderness support organization in northern Colorado. His passion for preserving the outdoors motivated him to form an organization that would make a difference.

The important thing in retirement that I've come to realize is that I had to reinvent myself. As a diplomat overseas, I was on duty twenty-four hours a day. I was always the representative of the United States of America. That was who I was. That was my whole persona. When I retired, that whole persona flew away. I have watched some of my former colleagues hang out in the Washington, DC area or in other capitals around the world, still trying to exist on the fringes of the diplomatic community. I realized I didn't want to do that, and my ex-wife and I moved to Colorado. That was a long way from Charles the diplomat.

I had to reinvent myself and I'm so glad I was able to do that. That just opened up a whole new area for me to develop myself in. It's really almost a second life.

I was very fortunate because I really retired at a little over age fifty. It was at a time when the Foreign Service was trying to get rid of some of the upper ranks of the pay scale. The sweeteners were wonderful, and I was given six months of full pay with no work to figure out what I wanted to do with the rest of my life. It was pretty much during that six-month period that I realized, 'I'm going to go do something entirely different. I'm going to be a different person.' I thought about how I could use what I do or my contacts to make money. I basically settled on starting a birdwatching tour company based in Southern Africa.

When I was posted in Southern Africa—in both Zimbabwe and Zambia—I spent a lot of my free time in the bush and became very interested in birds. I've always watched birds, but I started keeping a list and became very enamored with the birds of Southern Africa. I really became a birder.

I figured there was a good opportunity there for somebody to do tours to Southern Africa. I had the contacts down there to pull it off. And it worked well.

I launched that about a year after my retirement. It was 1994, when South Africa opened up. That was the year Nelson Mandela was elected. They had free and fair elections. The apartheid era had ended. Suddenly, Americans could all go with a good conscience to South Africa. There are a lot of good birds out there for international birdwatchers to see, and my business just mushroomed.

Starting the business was done, a little bit, by the seat of my pants. I knew how to run things. I put together an informal business plan and realized that I could probably make some money. It took a lot more care and feeding of clients than I really wanted to do. Some clients were very nice people. I had some difficult people. You really have to hold people's hands, especially if they're going off to Africa. I didn't particularly care for that part of the business. I had to devote many hours to this, and the returns were low. But I did make some money on it. Most of the money I made I put back into the business, just trying to make it grow.

I'd been doing it all out of my home by myself. Within four years I had to make a decision about either borrowing money and adding people or scaling it back.

At that point, I decided to scale it back, because I had a comfortable pension. I didn't really want to go and take the risk of borrowing money. The travel business margins are so slim. I decided it probably wasn't something I really wanted to pursue forever.

Then the American Birding Association came along and said, 'Would you like to run our tour program on a half-time basis?' I basically phased out my company and went to work for them for two years. I did that and then I really haven't earned a dime since.

At the same time that I was starting the birding business here, I was also volunteering for the Forest Service. Through the Forest Service, I was a volunteer backcountry ranger. I really got to know the wilderness area west of Fort Collins in Colorado. I learned basically what one needs to do to teach 'leave no trace' and build a trail and clean up fire rings and all that kind of stuff that a ranger would do. It included teaching visitors how to use the wilderness without impacting it.

I was a direct volunteer for two years. They gave me basic law enforcement training—not to carry a gun, but to write tickets and so on. I did that.

That place had gone from three full-time people and thirty seasonals dealing with wilderness and trails down to one full-time person and two seasonals in the course of two years. I was one of those two seasonal employees.

As an ex-federal employee, I understood a lot about how the federal government budgeting and funding process works. I realized that that money was never going to come back to the Forest Service in any way like it had been. They were not going to be able to care for these beautiful wilderness areas in northern Colorado that were under the jurisdiction of these ranger districts here. I went to the district ranger and I said, 'What if I tried to found a wilderness support organization?' They really encouraged me to do that, because they too could see the handwriting on the wall. They were just not going to have the manpower anymore to do these things.

Providing supportive contacts, guidance, and teaching in the wilderness really motivated me to try to see what I could do to help protect these beautiful areas. I set about putting together this organization. I got a lawyer friend to look it all over and make a few tweaks here and there. Basically, I did it all and assembled the building blocks of this organization. It was incorporated in 1996. I enlisted a friend who knew a lot of people in town. He helped me put together a really good first board of directors. It is almost twenty-four years ago now since we incorporated, and it has over three hundred members. It still is being run entirely by a volunteer board—no paid staff. That's the way I've set it up. Basically, we need a budget of about fifteen to twenty thousand dollars a year to run it.

We're doing a whole lot of things down there. I've been participatory in getting some of this stuff set up. Teaching 'leave no trace' on the trails, taking disadvantaged inner-city kids out in the woods for a day. A lot of stuff like that. We serve the desires of the Forest Service.

If I look at my life and consider what my greatest accomplishments have been, founding Poudre Wilderness Volunteers is really the most stellar thing.

The Forest Service rented llamas for the summer. I learned how to be a *yamico*, which is a llama handler. You learn to be a yamico by just working with somebody who has the skills. 'Here's your llama. Here's how to saddle it up and pack it and what its requirements are.' I got pretty skilled at it.

We cooked this thing up to do a llama trek for blind people. We had a sighted guide and a blind person. They were attached to each other by a long rope. At the end of that rope was the llama, who carried all the gear. The sighted guide would tell them everything that was coming along on the trail. There's a rock here and a root there, and don't lean to the right, you'll hit a tree. That was fun. It was five nights in the wilderness.

Llamas are great. The Forest Service had a llama by the name of Badger, and Badger was strong. He could haul anything, but he was cantankerous and occasionally would spit at you. Somebody told me at some point, 'If a llama ever does that to you, spit right back.' I did that at Badger and he never spat at me again. I had to assert my dominance.

I was with this blind woman. I was her guide one year. We came across a beautiful bed of columbine. I stopped and said to her, 'Joni, let's have a look at this.' We both got down on our knees and she held a columbine flower in her hand and she started to cry. She said, 'Some time ago someone gave me a columbine pressed in plastic and I've had it hanging in my window at home. I've never been able to tell what it was really like, and now here I can feel it, smell it, and I can feel its shape.' It was very touching.

Several times we helped the neighboring rancher move cattle both from winter pasture up to the mountains, and then in the fall, rounding them up and bringing them back down. I remember that I was dirty and wearing an old beat-up cowboy hat. I was pushing these cows up the road on my big quarter horse and we were blocking traffic. The traffic was going by really slowly. I remember parents pointing me out to a kid, saying, 'Look, there's a real cowboy.' My thought was, 'You should have seen me four or five years ago when I was riding in a black limousine with the American flag on the fender.'

18

GIG WORKING: A NEW MODEL FOR RETIREES

"You meet all kinds of people in all different walks of life."

> **Paul finds rideshare to be an enjoyable and low-stress way to work. He especially enjoys the riders.**

This stage of my life is interesting now because I still spend a lot of time 'working,' but it's only because I choose to work. Now my life feels really relaxed. I don't feel much pressure anymore. To me, that's retirement. I work almost as many hours as I used to, but I don't have the pressure. I can sleep in if I want, or I can do the things that I do to keep busy. It's pretty relaxed.

I started doing the rideshare just because it filled my hours. There are three rules that I'd say someone should go by if they want to do rideshare. Number one, you have to treat it like a business. Number two, you have to definitely like to drive. And three, you definitely can't have an ego, because people are not always friendly and are sometimes dismissive of you. I feel like I've driven according to these, and I find the work very good. I do it part time. I do it when I feel like it, so it's actually been fun. It gives me the chance to talk to people every day.

You talk to so many people, so many things that people do in life, so many different ideas. You get to tell your same stories over and over again. It's been very interesting. Money-wise, it's worth twenty-five or thirty thousand dollars a year if you do it part time. It's not a big moneymaker. But it definitely pays for vacations, pays for eating out, pays for the cars.

My favorite part of it is the passengers themselves. I was up in Blackhawk, which is an area close to me. I picked up a couple of 'professional ladies.' They got in the back of my car, and it became obvious right away that they were professional ladies because they asked me if I needed their services. They were up at the plastic surgery clinic. One of the ladies had just had a complete face peel. They asked me a couple of questions. I said, 'No, I'm happy. I just want to drive you!' They were very nice, but we did an epic drive. We stopped at three or four banks. We stopped at hotels. We stopped at restaurants. I was with them three or four hours during the trip. The funniest part about it was that they were calling their guys on the phone, right there in the car. They were booking themselves for whatever you call it . . . making their dates. It was my biggest ride, probably $150. They went everywhere. My wife was out with some of her friends, and I called her and I said, 'Judy, I'm out here with two hookers.' When I do take a really lovely woman, that's always a bonus. I get to take some really good-looking women. Where else would a nice, good-looking woman talk to me? They talk to me. They're nice. But the catch is, if I tell my wife about the ride, I have to give those fares to her.

You meet all kinds of people who come from all walks of life. It's always interesting when you get repeat customers. It's off-putting in the sense that these repeat customers can be like friends, but if they stop using you, your friend is just gone.

I've felt uncomfortable a few times but never really unsafe. Only once did I have to stop the car and tell this drunk passenger, 'Get out of my car.' That's been pretty good.

It's neat for this stage of my life. It's kind of retesting my driving skills. I know I'm not as good as I used to be. I tend not to drive at night anymore, and I particularly wouldn't do that if it was a drizzly night. You can modify what you want to do with this job.

19

BUILDING A WHOLE NEW CAREER: FOCUSING ON HER OWN AGE GROUP

"I've created a whole new career for myself, kind of a retirement career, and I love it."

Slowing down in retirement? That's simply not Elizabeth's way. She did her research, she got some in-depth knowledge about aging, and she began to apply it. She became an opinion leader in her field.

She shares that knowledge with interested seniors by writing books and articles, lecturing, counseling, doing webinars, and sharing information on social media. This whole new career has energized her and given her an important mission in life, that of helping seniors who will benefit from her knowledge.

A further test of her resilience and perseverance came at a critically busy time in the development of her new career. Elizabeth had to deal with the loss of her home in the Tubbs fire.

would say this stage of my life is interesting, sometimes exciting. Certainly not quiet. Sometimes it feels like I'm busier at this stage in my life than I've ever been at any other stage of my life. I've made it that way.

I've created a whole new career for myself—it's kind of a retirement career, and I love it. I just love what I'm doing. It keeps me buoyed up every day. When I'm doing something related to that, I'm at my happiest.

I started my company back in 2011. I did retirement coaching in tandem with my consulting work for three years. When we transitioned to our retirement location, I let the consulting work go and went full time into coaching people who are going into retirement. I just couldn't continue maintaining both activities at the same time.

I got involved with studying aging and retirement. I pretended like I was back in school again. I did the research. I researched what anthropologists knew about aging people in societies, what other cultures did, and what our culture did two hundred years ago.

Studying was the first thing. The next stage was talking to anybody who would sit still and listen about aging and retirement. I often ask them, 'What do you plan as you get older? Where are you planning to live? What are you planning to do?' Some of them will say things like, 'I don't know, I'm just going to see what happens.' It seemed like there were a lot of old people in denial. There's so much denial about getting old and the fact that we're going to die. The more I get comfortable with aging, dying, what the choices are, and what they could be, I just find it so fascinating.

I don't know how you can talk about it without talking about aging and helping people prepare to age. That's where I deviate from some of my colleagues who are just talking about retirement. It's part of a bigger picture. It's like talking about first grade and ignoring the rest of school.

People need to get comfortable with the idea of death. It's going to happen to all of us. Most of us don't know when. Death is part of life. We all have to get comfortable with the death of our friends. People talk about a 'good death.' I think that's valid. I think we all should think about what makes a good death for us. Who do we want to have around us, if we're able to have some choice in that? Where do we want to die? Many people say, 'I want to die at home,' and that's not very realistic, especially if the person hasn't planned very well.

But it's hard to plan for death. You don't know when it's going to come or by what hand. Maybe it will be cancer or dementia or maybe it will be a heart attack. Maybe you'll get hit by a bus. We just don't know. I think people should at least think about it and begin to talk to their families about it.

People have responded really positively to what I'm doing, and a lot of people have told me, 'You really opened my eyes to something that I was just blind to. I just wasn't thinking ahead and now I am.' Others have said, 'Wow, you have really stumbled onto something very important. You go, girl.' That was some encouragement.

It was in 2015 that I got really serious about writing a book. That kept me real busy. The messages in the book are upbeat. I spend a lot of time in the book talking about how to have an interesting, exciting, comfortable third act. Life after sixty-five is going to go on longer for many of us.

I view my work on aging as giving back. There are a lot of people out there who have said, 'Your book has helped me so much to understand what I'm facing later in life.' That feels good. It feels like I'm giving back.

I really believe that when you are starting in a new field it's important to join professional organizations that will help you network and learn, and will support what you're doing. I joined my first professional aging organization. The contacts I made there led to my first being part of a group book, where I played a large role. Then, ultimately, that led to good contacts for writing my own book. A lot of the people that blurbed the book for me, I met through that organization. It has led to tremendously positive things.

I guess if I had my druthers, I'd be working more. I think I'd be working more if I didn't have my husband, which of course I'm glad I have. I'm always aware of how much time I'm taking from us to do that. I'm really glad that he's got a lot going on. He can be in his office doing his thing. I'll be in my office doing my thing.

We were among many thousands of people who lost homes in the Tubbs fire; 5,500 homes were lost in Santa Rosa, so that's probably 15,000 to 20,000 people who were essentially made homeless for a while. You don't know how much resilience you have until something like that happens. You use some resources, tap into some storehouse of energy, knowledge, and mental capacity to get through it, and you're on autopilot. When I look back on it, I'm satisfied with how we responded. It seemed obvious, the thing to do. We just grabbed the dog and got in the old SUV that was sitting outside and drove away.

Our plan before the fire happened was not much different than our plan now. We just had to change houses. I really don't think the fire had any impact on our retirement plans or how we saw our life. We didn't make any major changes in anything. We just picked up the pieces, put our life back together, and kept on chugging on.

Because my husband and I do not have kids and we really don't have any nearby family, we are planning to move into a continuing care retirement community, probably in about ten years.

20

FLOW OF ACTIVITIES: UNCERTAINTY ABOUT WHAT'S NEXT

"I'm probably going to find something I like, but will that last?"

> During his work life, Chris was no stranger to reinventing himself. What those changes had in common was that the opportunities came to him without his seeking them out.
>
> Retirement has been different. The new ideas and activities have not shown up with the same certainty. His blend of work and philanthropic activities has only partially satisfied his pursuit of interesting activities.

The one word I would use to describe this stage of my life is 'confusing.' I'm physically and mentally just as capable as I was before. But all of the things I used to do that filled up my time and made it intellectually stimulating and made my life really fun are going away.

My career has had a lot of major shifts. My first job was as a professor of chemistry, and that was a planned career. My second job was president of the university, but that was not planned. I had no intention of being a university president. My third job was Big

Pharma, where I became a pharma exec. It happened, but I didn't plan it. My fourth profession was being a biotech CEO. I didn't plan that. My fifth profession was being a venture capitalist and I didn't plan that either.

It's part of the uncertainty of trying to do what I'm doing. I have this intuitive confidence that it'll keep on going, but it's the uncertainty. This isn't a cash issue. It's just a matter of interest. I believe I'll eventually find things that I like to do, but I don't know for sure.

Three main things are happening now: One, on a very selective basis I am helping companies get financed. I'm helping them with the business plan, with the strategy, with the staffing, with finding VCs who might be able to finance them. It's stuff I've done before and it's easy. I get to pick which companies I'm interested in. It's usually friends. When I help them, I take them to VCs who I like and trust. I don't have to go to all twenty-five or thirty VCs around the country. For me, it's more efficient, but it's also much, much more satisfying.

My second activity is the wind-down at the venture capital firm, helping out a few last companies.

My third activity is doing fundraising for nonprofits. I have an interest in music, and I have become involved with the Colorado Music Festival.

I'm really not sure what else I'm going to do in retirement. Things keep popping up, but I can't be sure that they're going to continue to pop up. Will I ever see another company I like enough to help get financed? I don't know, but I don't want to play golf all day. I feel a little bit like I'm coasting.

21

LEADERSHIP OF THE SCIENCE OF PLAY: IS THAT WORK OR PLAY?

"When you study a subject deeply, and the subject itself produces rewards, it's a pretty good life."

Stuart has devoted his life to leadership in the science of play. In his retirement, that calling continues, but he has adapted his activities to be more selective regarding those things he most enjoys.

Act Three describes the current stage of my life. During Act One, reproduction is the main thing. Act Two is a sense of professional competency. Act Three is what's been left over from the previous acts. And it's been pretty rich. I'd say, 'Go ahead and find whatever is your calling.' I just want to be able to hear the calling and respond to it. I feel very fortunate to have a sense of calling and that the calling has continued to nourish me.

I had a background as a boy with an extremely playful father and extended family. I would say I was grounded in a culture of play.

Most adults feel like they've lost their playful attitude, and finding it seems to be an important part of regenerating retirement. You need to find something that works for you, whether it's a game, gardening, hiking, or reading novels. There are all kinds of different patterns and paths.

Much of what I've been chasing for the last fifty-plus years has been an in-depth knowledge of play itself. Whether it's animal play, human play, play in the brain, or play in the cosmos—it just has to do with play. When you study a subject deeply and the subject itself produces rewards, it's a pretty good life.

You need the sense that you understand what works for you. I can think now of my playing tennis from age sixty-five to eighty-five with a guy named Jim. We would look at each other across the tennis court and laugh because we weren't very good. We'd heckle each other and just really have a great time. We've played together three times a week for fifteen years or so.

You begin to see the differences between a person who has ample play in their life and someone who's seriously play-deprived. I was standing in line at a pharmacy a couple of weeks ago and listening to the people in line. Everybody was waiting to get their medicine, and some of the people were chatting with each other in an amicable way. Others were more like 'Aren't they going to hurry up? What the hell is the matter?'

I enjoy a lot of activities. I got up at 5:30 this morning. I couldn't wait to get into Dan Siegel's book on self-organizing systems, because it's just so interesting.

On Monday night, I get together with a group of men. We've been getting together since 1989 and there are twelve of us now. It's called Carmel Men's Group and it's a very rich experience. Each guy brings to the table the totality of his life. We know one another's souls and we back each other up. That's really important to me. We meet every other week and one of us hosts a dinner. That's a very meaningful rhythm to be in, and is a very important part of my sense of self and life.

I have a great bond with my nineteen-year-old granddaughter, Mia. She is a delight and a very good gymnast. She did very well in the Division I Gymnastics Finals at the NCAA Championships. I get a joyful sense of continuity with Mia. She's really interested in play. She talks about her gymnastics, loving to compete because it's fun and a great opportunity. I would have been scared out of my mind if I'd been in front of six thousand people doing gymnastics for the NCAA finals in Fort Worth. She wasn't. She had a really good time. There is a sense of a continuity legacy. She's a step above where any of the rest of us would be if we were at the same time in her life, and I think I've influenced her in some good way. There is joy and laughter in that sense of continuity. It's really very special.

22

FINDING AUTONOMY: WORKING WITH A NEW APPROACH

"Shit, the frustration is too great. I don't want to do this anymore. Okay, I'm just going to do my own stuff."

Maurice wanted more independence in his work as a documentarian. For thirty-five years, he had been "hired help" doing projects for bosses. He helped those bosses win four Emmys with his work, but still something was missing.

In this stage of his life, he has decided to go it alone. He has his own documentary project in Gaza. Retirement for Maurice is doing documentary work, but he has the freedom now to choose the topic and do the work his own way. Independence is the new joy he has found in retirement.

His work in Gaza has also introduced him to local artists with whom he continues to explore new opportunities.

Maurice is at a crossroads about what to do next.

think the three aspects of life are your relationships, what you do to earn a living, and your lifestyle choices. I try to look at it intellectually, like a Venn diagram. That's when there are three circles that all partially overlap.

A perfect Venn diagram is when you have everything in balance. I think I've always had two of them in place, but never seemed to quite get all three. I've either had an incredible job and an interesting lifestyle but not a good relationship, or a really good relationship but I haven't had the lifestyle that I wanted. I still feel I'm on this quest to try to get everything in balance.

I was working on a really big project for Discovery Channel for about two and a half years. We shot probably four hundred hours of footage. They wanted to focus on the adventure aspect of our subject, but I didn't think that was the real story. That was it for me. I said, 'Shit, the frustration of this is too great. I don't want to do this anymore.' I had previously been doing other people's projects as a cameraman, narrator, or producer. I knew the field. I knew the dynamics. I had enough confidence in myself. Working on my own wasn't that different.

This big change came when I had a serious cancer. I was out of commission for about a year. Historically, it was a traumatic time, especially in the Middle East. It was when the first invasion of Gaza happened by Israel. I was laid up and not really able to get out of bed at the time. I was watching a lot of television news, and the injustice of it just incensed me. For me, personally, it was a humanitarian issue. I saw that the real story was how people's lives were affected. How would the people of this tiny little country or territory rebuild?

I said, 'Okay, I'm just going to do my own stuff. I'm going to try to raise the money to do projects and just do my own work.' At that point, I transitioned from working for others to working on my own project. I was able to get a small grant from a foundation and I attempted to travel to Gaza.

There was a delegation from the Rachel Corrie Foundation. Rachel Corrie was a young American volunteer who went to Gaza to help the residents. While protecting a home from being bulldozed, she was run over by a bulldozer and killed. Her parents took on the cause and started a foundation to publicize the situation in Gaza. One of the things that they wanted to do was to bring small delegations of academics and journalists into Gaza to see what the situation was like. A reporter from the *Washington Post* and I embedded ourselves with their delegation. This was a perfect way to enter Gaza, so eventually we got in.

I started working with Oxfam and a couple of other NGOs. I met with human rights organizations and visited refugee camps. I ended up staying in Gaza for nearly two and a half years.

I first did profiles of seven families in Gaza—this kind of depicted a whole cross-section of people and gave a sense of what it's like under siege, hearing it from their point of view. A single mother, the mayor of the town of Rafah, a couple of artists, a farmer.

Everybody in Gaza—from the prime minister to somebody in abject poverty—wanted to tell their story. They knew that I hadn't come in with preconceptions of how this story should be told. I wanted to hear from them and let them express themselves.

The interviews I do are very much like we're having a conversation. I set up a good quality camera at eye level, and we just sit and talk for maybe an hour or two.

When you're out there, you have to believe in fate and that you're going to be okay. You have to believe that you're doing good work, and that God will watch you. Also, when you go to these places, you meet just incredibly wonderful people who want to protect you and take care of you. You feel afraid, but it's complicated. It's not a fear. It's like:

'I'd better be careful. They just bombed this neighborhood yesterday. Maybe it's a good idea not to go to that neighborhood today.'

I was staying in Gaza in a classic bed-and-breakfast kind of place. It's owned by a Palestinian, but the whole place has a real English feel to it. It's walled and there's a really nice garden restaurant that could hold its own with any restaurant in the world. That's where I was staying.

One night about 10:00 or 10:30 I had just gotten into bed. I heard this explosion. It was the loudest explosion I had ever heard in my entire life. It rattled my windows and broke some windows downstairs. It was a bomb that hit right next to the hotel and completely flattened the houses and buildings there. That shook me. I ran out with my camera. There was just a hole in the ground and it was pretty scary.

I toured the documentary to college campuses and churches and community groups all over the US and UK. The film presentation was free, but I was able to support the tour by asking for donations. It didn't raise a lot; I'd always raise at least two hundred, three hundred, four hundred dollars at any given tour stop.

The other thing that I was doing was selling posters. One of the characters in the documentary is an artist whose name is Malak. She's amazing. She's only a young girl of twenty and an amazing artist. What I was doing was selling her posters. That's where I got an income. That's how I supported the trip.

Malak describes her work by saying she's trying to tell the soul of Gaza through the eyes of the women she paints. Not only is she a gifted painter, she's also a poet. She has this line that I think is just an amazing line. The poem goes, 'When peace dies, embrace it. It will live again.' That's her message.

Malak got a full scholarship to study in Istanbul. She's there now. She and I were talking about creating a traveling art exhibition of artwork from Gaza and taking it to all the major capitals. I think the art project has a real possibility of finding support. We took the project to the UN, and the UN liked the idea a lot. They said they don't have any money, but could maybe give us a letter of endorsement which we could then take to the foundations.

Pretty much everybody said that they really liked the documentary. It raised a lot more questions about why Gaza exists as it does. How can Israel keep a siege going for just this nominal reason of security? I said, 'This is really a valid question.' I said, 'Okay. I can't answer that question, because it's a mystery to me as well.' I traveled the world for another nine months trying to answer that question, 'Why Gaza?' I got lots of answers.

It's explained now with the re-edited documentary. All the content is done for the re-edit. I need to raise about another fifteen or twenty thousand dollars to finish it. It needs quality technical work done, so it can be shown.

The decision I have to make is whether I stay here in California and finish the Gaza documentary. I could just do another crowdsourcing site or keep writing foundation grants until I get the money to finish it. Work is so much of my life that it's almost become a dominant thing. When I'm talking about one of the things that I may or may not do, it's a big decision. I have to confess, I need to make a major decision.

I got back from Gaza. I got all my finances sorted out. I got my health sorted out. I went back to Kaiser to make sure that the cancer wasn't back. I'm free of cancer. I'm physically not perfect, but I'm in pretty good shape.

I have a good camera kit. I can still travel. I still feel like I want to be out in the world, but at seventy-five, I have to worry more about my health than I ever did before.

I'm thinking about going back to places where there is no health coverage or where your life can be at risk. I would go into Syria or

Chechnya. I would go anywhere. It doesn't frighten me. What does frighten me is getting sick there. Also, I've reached a point where I realize I've been traveling almost all my life.

I've had some interesting relationships, but I've never been married and I don't have any kids. Relationships could be part of my decision-making. That would change things drastically if I decide I want to go out and create a relationship and find somebody, go online and try to meet somebody.

In all honesty, at seventy-five, I don't want to say I'm a curmudgeon, but I don't mind being by myself. I don't feel like I need somebody. I've always been very independent. I don't need to feel like if I wanted to take a walk on the beach, I have to be hand in hand with somebody. I'm perfectly happy taking a nice long walk on the beach by myself. When you're in a relationship, you have a responsibility to that relationship. When I did try to do the normal lifestyle with a house and a nine-to-five job, I really wasn't very happy.

A lot of decisions that I've made over my life have happened organically. Something will come up. In the past, when I've said to myself, 'Shit, what am I going to do?' I get a phone call. 'Are you interested in working on this project?' Or I meet somebody and I move in with them. Something happens. I feel like psychologically I'm ready for something to happen.

In the developed world there are two kinds of people. There are people who are either what I would call 'nesters' or 'flyers.' Nesters are people who have to have a home as their security blanket. It's their grounding. Everything revolves around home base. Flyers feel they must go see the world. I've had the philosophy that being a flyer is genetic. If you're born with those genes, then you can't be anything else. For better or worse, I've got the flyer genes. I'm just not happy to park. Practicality now, at seventy-five, raises its head and says, 'Do I just keep doing this until I have a heart attack or fall off a cliff or, God forbid, somebody shoots me?' I don't know. I don't have an answer. I really don't have an answer.

I have had an amazing life. I have no regrets, except maybe some stupid little things, but overall, no. I couldn't see doing it another way.

23

FILLING HIS CAREER SPACE: TESTING LIMITS WITH SOMETHING NEW

"There was going to be something missing that I had to replace."

As he was phasing down his work career, John identified some things he enjoyed in his career that he wanted to continue into his retirement. He set about an organized process to examine his alternatives.

would describe this stage of my life as very much unplanned.

For a while, it was uncomfortable, and I'd sit around and go, 'What do I have to do tomorrow?' Then I'd go, 'I don't have to do anything tomorrow.' I like that. That's one half of it, but the other half is that I know that there is a clock running. I'd never paid attention to that clock in the past. Every once in a while I go, 'Wait a minute, the clock is running and I don't know how long I'm going to last.'

I don't know when I'm going to lose my marbles and I have to get as much out of my remaining time as I possibly can—not for any altruistic reasons, but just because I want to get as much out of life as I can. On one hand, I don't have to think about what I'm going to do tomorrow. On the other hand, I really spend a good deal of effort making sure that I get the best out of every day. Now, defining the best out of every day is a different thing.

You've got to go *to* something. I look at my life simplistically and say I love exercising and cycling and sailing and that kind of stuff. I love traveling. I love being with my family. But there is a missing piece.

If you took my previous career out of the mix, there'd be a huge thing missing. My career was all about challenge. It was the challenge of problem solving and doing business and finding ways to make money. I was hanging on to my career as a consultant until I found something that could fill the void that leaving it would create. I redefined the gap. I looked at lots of different things, philanthropic stuff and social ventures, things like that.

I've redefined what I was looking for in this final phase of my life. I realized that I wanted to do some business. I wanted to challenge my business mind. I wanted to learn some new stuff and have some fun, because I thought that would be part of the challenge. I wanted to reconnect myself with Cincinnati. The money wasn't the number one thing, but money is a nice way for me to keep score.

I have a friend who I've known for quite some time who is part of this group, Queen City Angels, an angel investing group. I knew about Queen City Angels, but I know next to nothing about angel investing. This is all investing in early stage start-ups. They focus primarily on technology with companies that are in the region. They have roughly sixty members in the group. They put money into this thing. The sixty people are all really interesting people from Cincinnati.

I wondered if I could make a contribution. I thought their requirements might be more than I'd be willing to contribute. I was sitting there on the fence. I went to talk to the principals about it. They don't know what my contribution will be, but it's obvious to them that I'll make a contribution, just given what my CV looks like.

I ended up sitting in on some of their meetings and thought, this just looks like fun. It's fun to hear them talk, and they've got a good sense of humor. The job has tremendous flexibility, so if I'm in town I can dive into it and have some fun. Then I've got no problem walking away from it until the next time I'm in town. So that's a really good deal.

I attended a planning meeting. I was stopping people every five minutes, 'Sorry, explain that to me . . . what's that? How does that work? I don't get it.' I was dumber than I thought I was when it came to financial evaluation tools. There is so much that I don't know. This is a language that I don't speak.

I know how to run a P&L, but the investment language is all new stuff. I now sit and just try to keep track of terms. Half the time I listen to what they're saying. The other half I'm googling the terms they're talking about. I don't know any of this shit.

I did learn that I have value because of my consulting experience. I can look at a business and ask whether the business makes any sense. I was one of the few people saying, 'Do you think this thing could make any money? Or will it get any traction with a consumer?' I realized that I don't have to become a financial expert, because that's the value of a diverse team. I really believe that. I can contribute in my corner from the get-go while I develop at least a passing knowledge of some of the other stuff.

Queen City Angels fills a very nice gap. It's kind of fun. I'm always trying to balance my life.

24

BACK TO SCHOOL: NEW SKILLS FOR HER OUTDOOR FOCUS

"When I knew retirement was on the horizon, I went back to school and got a Master's in Sustainable Studies and Environmental Management."

Eleanor shifted gears in retirement. She wanted to pursue her passion for the outdoors but felt she needed more training. She took the challenge of reinventing herself by adding new skills through extensive university-based training.

She was a high school teacher, then an administrator, which included a role as the advisor to the school's environmental club. By the time of her retirement at age sixty-six, she had her Masters in Sustainable Studies and Environmental Management. She was ready. She had prepared herself for this next stage of her life.

With her newly acquired skills and experience, she has become a freelance writer, covering environmental stories. Her work until now has been gratis, but she would welcome a paycheck for it one day.

She explores other activities and is still working on finding the right balance for all of them.

'Exploring' is the word I'd use to describe my current situation. I'm trying to figure out what I most want to do next. I have a lot of interests, and so I've been dabbling and seeing where that takes me. Although I'm trying to narrow it down, my interests keep expanding rather than narrowing.

I was a high school teacher, then an Associate Principal at a high school. I was also the environmental club advisor. I've always been, for the East Coast, considered a bit earthy—a crunchy-granola type. I've always been concerned about how we live on the planet.

I was sixty-six when I retired. I have three adult kids who are all living out here in Portland. I was the only one left on the East Coast, so it was a no-brainer. If there were going to be grandkids coming, I wanted to be part of their lives. In fact, there is one coming. I've got one due in the next three weeks.

I also want to put a little bit of knowledge from the work I did with the environmental club to good use. I'd rather be outside for my next thirty years than inside. What can I do that will get me there? Writing can be done anywhere. If I go visit a national park for a few weeks and then come home and write about it, I can do that from home. In my brain, it came together well.

When I knew retirement was on the horizon, I went back to school and got a Masters in Sustainable Studies and Environmental Management. I was thinking that I would do freelance writing for different outdoor organizations, foundations, national parks, and other places like that. I started taking those courses and got my Master's. I went each summer and volunteered in a different national park or recreation area and did some writing for them.

My attitude toward the outdoors is that there's just so much I don't know. I have a basic understanding of ecological systems and the unintended consequences of planting species that later become invasive. Each place I go is so full of its own biological and zoological wonders. I feel so puny next to it all. There's so much out there to learn. I let others be the experts and I see myself as a generalist, both in experience and in what I write about. I'm never going to be a zoologist or a botanist, but I can write about the big picture, which is important for people to understand. So much of what we're experiencing with climate change and the deniers here in this country is because they just don't have an understanding of the systemic nature of the problem.

Here in Portland, I've taken two classes from Oregon State University online. One was for Master Naturalist and one for Master Gardener. This Master Naturalist course was all online except for a six-day fieldwork portion. I did my fieldwork in the High Desert. I thought those courses would get me out meeting like-minded people in outdoor settings and I could feed that part of me.

I've also volunteered out on the Oregon coast, helping pull invasive Scotch broom, which has taken over the dunes. The pulling of invasive species feels like a Sisyphean task. You can clear this entire fifty-by-fifty-foot plot of a particular weed, and come back in two weeks and it's all back again. I guess what I'm saying is, planting definitely felt better than pulling.

Southwestern coastal Oregon has several sheets of dunes, and they're shrinking because the forest is encroaching. As a result, it's now preventing the dunes from doing what dunes do, which is blow, move, and shift. Because they're not blowing and shifting, the forest has been able to encroach around the edges and even in the center of the dunes. The Forest Service has been charged with preserving the historical and the natural elements of the dunes for the enjoyment of the American public. The question is, How do we preserve the dunes and let people ride their off-road vehicles and let naturalists protect endangered species like the plover?

We're trying to meet all these different needs of all these different stakeholders. They've come together in this organization called the Oregon Dunes Restoration Collaborative. They wanted us to make a film that would inform people about why they don't want the dunes to be anchored and why a forest isn't always the thing you want to grow. Sometimes you want dunes. I wrote the script for this little eight-minute film that they have made. They've been talking about making this film for a long time and they just didn't know where to start. I said, I think you need to start with a script. I wrote them a draft and took the feedback and fixed it up. Then they did the filming and the splicing.

As of now, all my writing has been gratefully accepted by the places I volunteered with, but I haven't got any money to show for it. That's okay, because my teacher's pension is quite ample. Still, it would be really lovely if somebody wanted to buy one of my stories.

Over the last several years, I've also taken up mosaic making. I've taken several weeklong courses in mosaics in different places like Italy, Tucson, and Chicago. The mosaic making is also outdoors. I teach garden mosaic making at the community garden I work at. Each time I do it, I get this good feeling. People are enjoying themselves. I'm sharing with them something they want to learn. I'm trying to weave that feeling into what I'm doing, and maybe that's where the reward will come from.

A lot of people keep saying, 'You should charge for these classes. You could support yourself on this.' I don't want to, really, and I don't. Having been a teacher all my life, I'm good at teaching. I know how to set it up so people get it and can create something, but I also don't want to make it an everyday thing.

Back when I was in college, I went camping with my friends, and we would see these retirees driving their motor homes down the Blue Ridge Parkway of Virginia and North Carolina. I thought that looked like a great way to retire. It became a long-term vision for me. The year before I retired, I bought a car that could pull a trailer. Then the next year, I retired and I bought the trailer. It's small. It's fine for my size. If somebody's six feet and wanted to sleep in it, they'd have to be scrunched up. It probably wouldn't be comfortable for two people long term, but I can maneuver it myself and do the hookup. As my kids say, I'm badass. I've learned how to do all this stuff in my trailer.

I've been taking it to see different places. I like the campground because I can usually hook up to water and sometimes electricity. I've also taken it in the middle of an ungrazed portion of this cattle owner's land. I just pulled in and parked there with no amenities. You can do either. It's got a water tank that will last for a couple of days. It's pretty versatile. I've moved from Boston to Portland with it. I picked up my sister in Chicago and she came along with me.

This summer I went to Glacier National Park and Banff and Calgary. I've taken it all around central Oregon on the Sunday volunteer stint. It's helping me see the places I want to see and be outdoors.

Having been so career-oriented for most of my life, I do feel like I should have more focus. I'm also enjoying not having to get up every morning at six and rush off to work. I can pick what I want to do today, which has been wonderful.

Teaching, writing, and the environment are a skill set that I see as a unit. I haven't found one place that all of it can be applied to. I'm using several places.

I'm a generalist. That's maybe just where I need to be at this time. I've always wanted to know that I had this passion for something and just go for it, but I seem to have passions that are shallower but entertaining. That's the generalist in me. I need to come to terms with that, that I'm not the sort who's going to become an expert in one thing.

There is something about it not feeling quite right. I haven't been able to put my finger on what that is. I never went for a PhD because I really don't have the patience to become an expert in something. Instead, I've gone for a couple of Masters and a whole ton of other fun learning experiences. I'm okay with that, but maybe it's just that there's too much free time.

PART FOUR

LEISURE ACTIVITIES: HAVING FUN CAN BE SO MUCH FUN

R etirement is a time when we are liberated. We have choices. It's up to us to find what leisure activities are right for this stage of life. For some, that first year of retirement is a bit intimidating as new routines are developed. For others, there is a time of transition and experimentation and learning what they really want. Still others already have their leisure activities figured out and prioritized on their first day after finishing work.

You don't get sent to a penalty box if you get it wrong. Be open to some new ideas, but be quick to abandon those that do not bring you what you want.

The interviewees in this section are doing quite a range of leisure activities and have shown a tolerance for raising their limits. But in most of the stories, you will see some trial and error to get there. Although not mentioned in the interviews, there's also an important place for just having some down time, taking it easy, and maybe watching a Yankees game or reading a good book.

One of the interviews might give you a new leisure idea that is exactly right for you. Fly fishing, running a marathon, organizing a party, taking up painting. If one of the ideas strikes your fancy, go for it.

The more important takeaway from these interviews is that there are lots of choices. Your leisure activities during retirement can consist of simply expanding something you already like and want to do more of. Playing more golf could be ideal for you.

But the freedom of retirement gives you a wider range of choices. What could you do that would make your friends and kids ask, "Are you crazy? You've never done anything like that before."

Multitasking our leisure is an additional choice we all have. So if you are going to climb Kilimanjaro, you may choose to get a tattoo before you go.

25

UNLEASHING THE ARTISTIC:
DISCOVERING THE CREATIVE SIDE

"I realized I didn't want to do what I'd always been doing. My IT career was all analytical, systematic, rational skills. I felt that I'd underdeveloped my artistic, intuitive, conversational potential."

Steve retired at age fifty-five. His career had always been concentrated on analytical, left-brain matters. He's been wanting to exercise his creative right brain in retirement. That right brain is now in high gear across a range of activities.

He designs his retirement through introspection about what he wants for this stage of his life. He continually challenges himself to enrich his retirement by doing activities he has not done before. Music and painting have provided him inspiration and learning as he explores his creative side. In an extended visit to a Greek isle, his first gig as a soloist became a starting point for forming a community around music.

Everything you know about tells you that your life is over. It finished about ten years ago. I retired when I was fifty-five. I'm now sixty-five and I'm just waiting to die. Rationally, you know that probably there's active life until seventy-five, maybe eighty-five. My father's eighty-eight and he still plays in a band and he's learning baritone sax.

When you analyze it, you think, 'Wait a minute, don't I want to do something different? What about all that freedom that seemed to be on this side of the fence back when I was on the other side?' I think there's something I want to do. Of course, I don't know what it is because I'm too busy doing other things.

I realized I didn't want to do what I'd always been doing. My IT career was all analytical, systematic, rational skills. I felt that I'd underdeveloped my artistic, intuitive, conversational potential. I found it more rewarding to do a course in mentoring—coaching—and learn how to listen to people and ask questions. It's more rewarding because you feel you're making more important progress and doing the work that you've neglected for decades. For me, retirement has become more about filling the gap than trying to achieve more of the same stuff.

My wife does sort of lightweight counseling. I realized she has more to offer people. It's very attractive. She has a condition that I refer to as 'damp shoulders.' Often, the people she counsels she hardly knows. It's people that she's hardly met. I'm thinking that's very attractive.

The mnemonic I used for what I wanted to choose to do was AMP. It was Autonomy, Mastery, and Purpose. You've got to be building your own dream, not somebody else's. You've got to be doing something that you're good at, because we all need respect. It's got to be something worthwhile.

At one stage, having done nine weeks of training ourselves how to listen to somebody, we sat back to back silently and listened to each other. I was physically shaken and shocked by the depth and the correctness of what I had heard from the other person without looking or hearing anything. Listening is an amazing gift that we should all be trying to develop. Having spent my time learning how to intuitively interact with a computer and programs, I thought it's time I got involved with other people.

For a long time, I've been the singer at the front of a wedding band. The band is called Our Dad. All of my children play in this band, together with some other musicians. This is a very special band. We got invited to play at a sixtieth birthday party. I got to play in front of all the professional musicians in my extended tribe. Of all the people that this guy knew, he chose a band that doesn't have a recording contract. Yes, that's us. Amateurs. We've had quite a lot of accolades in that way—I feel that we're kind of like musicians' musicians. The music of Our Dad is very creative because we don't have any rehearsals. We rely purely on the relationship between the musicians, and their skills. Just celebrate and enjoy each other and forgive each other the mistakes and just carry on. It generates more love than you need, and it just spills out off the stage into the audience.

We rented a house for six months on the Greek island of Aegina. Suddenly we were thrown into this fantastic community that was growing faster than we could update our address book. We were meeting artists, craftsmen, musicians, people who work with refugees, activists working on food diversity, and just a fascinating array of people. We loved it.

When we went to Greece, we found this famous music bar called Proka. I tried something I hadn't done for fifty years, which is to sing solo. Bear in mind, I'm usually standing in front of a band, so it's not really a lot of work. When there are seven musicians, each person is responsible for making one-seventh of the music. But I had a go at this. It really took off. I found it very exciting, partly because it's different. The audience was very quiet and attentive and appreciative. In a wedding, let's not say you're competing with the audience, but they often have different things on their mind.

The community starts around the music. I ended up becoming a resident musician every Wednesday and Friday night. Music was the way in and I was making connections at all different levels. I became acquainted with everyone in the audience. I very quickly became friends with people that I was making music with. That's a very intimate activity, especially if you're at the level where you're improvising.

There was a Norwegian piano player in the bar. He took my arm on a quiet evening and asked me to come and sing. He was playing the piano with his head down and his eyes closed, just listening to me. I had no props, no microphone, and just got up and sang. We made music that way—just improvised jazz. If you've never done something like this, I have to say, it's really freeing. You're listening to somebody so intently to catch their mood and their expression of that mood, to lock into it at every detail. It's about as intimate as you can get with your clothes on with another human being. It's quite embarrassing if you're doing it with somebody of the same sex.

It's the kind of activity where you get to know somebody very deeply and very quickly. Somebody asked me if it is true that when you improvise when you make music, people can tell what you're like. I said it's much worse than that.

I was then invited into a group that sings ethnic Greek traditional music. They make their own instruments. They gather at night under the stars, watching the reflection of the moon go across the ocean. They sing and eat and dance and play until the sun comes up—yes, glorious.

We had gone to Malawi to provide some technical advice on projects in their refugee camp named Dzaleka. Somebody from our church married a guy from Burundi who is now in Malawi. He had been a refugee for the first twenty-seven years of his life in all the poorest countries of Africa. He turned out to be a musician. Music became the route to community. When we went there, we initiated a guitar school by taking a couple of guitars into the refugee camp.

We were on holiday about four years ago. My wife Mary got out her paintbrush and her paints, and I thought: I'd like to have a go at that. I made a drawing on a little book and I colored it in. I put it on Facebook, and people liked it. I thought: 'This is exciting. I'm getting approval from people for doing art.'

I developed it. After one year, I was doing a little art club. Somebody in the arts center liked the writing that I did on my pictures. He said, 'We need new signage above the doors in our arts center. If you could put four-inch letters above each door to say "stage door" and "theater" and "toilets," then we would give you a two-week gallery for free.'

I accepted the offer. Six months later, I did a two-week exhibition of my paintings and sold twenty-five pieces. I made nearly a thousand pounds (approximately $1,300). I was very happy with that.

One of the things I learned on the way was that I could actually mix my technical background to do computer modifications of the artwork. The old skills that I wanted to put behind me have actually crept in and helped push me forward, developing skills that I didn't know I had. I felt like I'd invented a new technique, which made me very proud and gratified.

Another thing that really bugged me when I left work was that our church had a meltdown, as many churches often do. I had to stop, take stock, and think: Do I want to go back to this church? Do I want to go back to a church in the same network? Do I even want to go back to an evangelical or even a Protestant church?

That started me on a journey to try and work out what I believe. It's very undermining. It's where you pull the carpet, the floorboards, and the foundations of your house away from beneath your own feet—maybe even the foundation of your marriage if it's based on your shared faith. For ten years, I have been reading theology and looking for people I could talk to about theology.

We're definitely looking to change more. Sometimes it comes where you're not looking for it. We went to Greece wanting to do painting and drawing and ended up realizing that there was a new avenue in music that is very rich and rewarding.

I've been accused of being a Renaissance man and I'm not sure why. I do think that retirement is a great opportunity. If you haven't thought about the breadth of your interests, it's a great opportunity to stop and take a think about that. It's easier than it seems: join a club, try something new, and suddenly, holding a pencil or a brush or reading a book is something you really like. You can go off in different directions.

26

MATURE VIEW OF SPORTS: CHAMPIONSHIP TENNIS IN YOUR SEVENTIES

"We know it doesn't affect our ego as much."

> **Tennis is an important part of Sally's retirement. Her focus and desire to win remains strong, but her attitude has shifted to one of gratitude for still being able to play.**

Tennis is something I just really enjoy. I look forward to it. Tennis is so good because you get great exercise, and it's not going full steam ahead all the time. You do little spurts. As far as your health, that's supposedly the best thing for your heart—to do high intensity and then get your heart rate back to normal intensity. That's what tennis does for you.

It's also wonderful because I only play doubles. There are three other people who are fun to visit with. It's a social arena that just fills your time up. I can't play as many days in a row as I used to. It just gets that social time and that physical exercise time in. It's just fun. With the game, you get your brain cells going. In doubles, you have to be really pretty smart to make sure that those two people over there are covering a lot of court. How are you going to get it in the spot where they ain't?

We have matches that are through the US Tennis Association. You can go from your neighborhood to regionals and all the way to Nationals. My teams have gone to Nationals quite a few times. It's exciting to play in the national USTA. We travel to a different city, and we get to stay in a hotel.

You have to be really focused. I have a friend who was really so competitive. She could manage it by talking through the whole match, which would drive some people crazy. I can't do that. I have to really focus and pay attention. It's a really nice balance to get to be really intense and focused, then laugh and shake hands when it's done. Then you find out about the people or you become friends with them.

I think when you're younger, you don't have the perspective of 'This outcome really doesn't matter. It's not earth-shattering.' At this point, it doesn't affect our ego as much. I played one time with a friend and we didn't do well. Afterwards, she cried and I thought, 'Oh my God. This is *tennis!*' It doesn't make any sense to be a senior and be crying over tennis. Tennis is a game. It's an enhancement of your life. It's not going to ruin my life at all if I lose once. I look at it as a learning experience. 'Okay, I lost. What did I do? How can I change that so that maybe we don't lose so badly next time?' I might even figure it out and win. I just feel like it's an enhancement to my life.

I think we're all grateful. When we're on the court, we're excited, because we have lots of friends who have knee issues or shoulder issues, or they've just given up. They go to golf or they play bridge. Most of us who play now, we're like, 'Wow. We're here. It's a beautiful day.' We enjoy one another.

27

FROM WINE COUNTRY TO KILIMANJARO: TAKING ON NEW CHALLENGES

"I'm finally in one piece again and with all these new joints, new knees and new hips, I wanted to celebrate by doing something really tough. I wanted to go climb Kilimanjaro."

Taking on new challenges is part of Donna's DNA. She began a successful journalism career in her mid-thirties and hasn't stopped exceeding expectations.

When she decided to retire, she knew she needed to find a way to spend her time that would enable her to learn something new, have fun, interact with people, and make enough money to maintain her lifestyle.

Donna's most recent test was a physical one: to climb Mount Kilimanjaro, the tallest mountain in Africa. Nothing was going to get in her way, not even several leg surgeries.

see my retirement as productive retirement because I'm only *half* retired. I'm just about to turn seventy-one, but I have to still work to keep the lifestyle I want. I like working because it gives me a reason to get up in the morning.

My boyfriend saw an ad for Wine Country tour guides. He said, 'Why don't you do this? It's part time and you're good with people.' And that's how I became a Wine Country tour guide. It's an easy gig, really. I only work two to three days a week. The people I drive around are in a great mood. I drive them to beautiful wineries and talk about wine. One of my favorite things about living in this area is how many absolutely gorgeous wineries there are in Napa and Sonoma. All of the guests say how beautiful these rolling hills are, with grapevines and roads going up and down the hills. Then we pull into these delightful wineries with beautiful old buildings and lots of history.

I didn't want to just drive people. I wanted to learn all about wine and the wineries. I feel that I'm more than a driver. I like to educate my guests about Wine Country. The guests all say I'm very informative. It's because I was a journalist and a researcher. It's more fun for me to find out a lot about winemaking, how wine grapes are grown, and why wine country produces such great wine. It's fun for me to give this little educational spiel during the day.

I've met some really interesting people from all over the world. I've gotten to witness two wedding proposals, which were very sweet and nice to be a part of.

Once there were some young lawyers and one nurse from San Francisco. They hired me because they wanted to party while I drove. They were doing cocaine in the back seat, and smoking pot. They wanted me to do cocaine, and I was like, 'Guys, I'm *driving*.' That was a wild day. They managed to drink wine at several stops in between doing the cocaine and the pot in the car.

Being a Wine Country tour guide definitely pays more than minimum wage. It is a part-time gig that's kind of cool and fun. I also like being my own boss. With this, you're never stuck in one location.

In the past four years, I have had both knees and hips replaced. I was really out of commission and couldn't be very athletic for the past three years because I was always getting over one surgery or another. When I got my second hip last year, I was finally all in one piece again. With all these new joints, new knees and new hips, I wanted to celebrate by doing something really tough. I wanted to go climb Kilimanjaro.

We picked Kilimanjaro because it's in Africa and because it's so iconic. My boyfriend is a mountain climber. He's done Whitney twice. He's climbed Rainier. He's climbed Mt. Hood. When I said, 'Hey, do you want to climb Kilimanjaro?' he was like, 'Yes. It's one of the seven summits.'

I trained a lot. I did a lot of six-hour hikes to prepare, because the best way to prepare for hiking is to do a lot of hiking. As the trip got closer, I thought, 'Oh my God, I hope I can do this.' But then I settled into the thought: I think I can do it. I'm just going to go with a good attitude. My friends said, 'My God, I can't believe you're doing this,' and I kept saying, 'I don't know if I can.' They thought it was a very brave thing to do, especially after so many leg surgeries.

The climb was six consecutive days of hiking—six hours a day. Everybody got really stinky after the second day. We had wet wipes, and I made my boyfriend take a wet wipe bath because, I said, 'I'm not sleeping in the same tent with you.' Sleeping on the ground in the tent was an endurance trial. It's not the most comfortable place, and after five nights it really gets old.

I thought the climb would be more scenic, but the landscape is kind of arid and desert-like. In these vast open spaces, I was pushing myself to my limit. I'd never done that much hiking in that short of a time. We didn't have problems breathing. We both took altitude-sickness pills, which I think helped. But I was just exhausted.

Once we got to base camp at altitude 15,400, I had a bad headache. I was disoriented. My blood pressure had climbed thirty points. I was shaking, and I thought there'd be no way I could do eleven hours to the summit feeling like this.

I did not make it to the summit. I was disappointed but I knew I wouldn't have made it. My boyfriend told me I probably would have gotten a couple of hours in and they would have had to take me back down. That would have been even more disappointing. So I made the right decision.

My boyfriend made it to the summit. He didn't need oxygen, but he said as he got closer to the top—at 19,341 feet—every step was really an exertion. They left at midnight and they didn't get to the summit until 7:00 a.m. The summit climb is designed so that you get there at sunrise and you get back down before dark. It means that you're climbing seven hours in the cold dark. At that altitude, it was about zero degrees, and he said it was very windy. Then, coming down, they were hit with an hour or two of snow. Oh, my God, it's really dangerous. You have to really be careful. When he got back from the summit and I took a good look at him, I realized I would never have made it. He actually started crying because he was so overwhelmed.

Attempting to climb Kilimanjaro was a wonderful experience. I've never done anything like it before.

I've had a good life. I've had a long and varied life. I'm probably going to live to be 101 like my Filipino dad. I don't know if I want to live that long, but I think I've got it in me, for sure.

28

FINALLY GETTING A TATTOO: CONNECTING WITH YOUR ARTISTIC SELF

"I've become surprisingly addicted to the idea of more tattoos."

> **Dave waited until his retirement years to get his first tattoo. It's been an artistic adventure for him.**

I am a child of the sixties. I'm definitely a little bit of a semi-radical type. I've always loved artwork. When I see people who have interesting tattoos, I see it as a form of art. While I'm not an artist personally, I have artists in my family. They include two of my kids, my wife, my uncle, my mom's brother, and my mom's second cousin. I've always appreciated art.

I've always viewed this tattoo thing as body art. I like Native American and Polynesian art. Most of the tattoos that spoke to me had to do with that kind of imagery. I probably went two or three years where, every couple of months, I'd spend three or four hours looking at different tattoo artists' sites. I just never quite saw anything that I wanted to imitate.

Then I met a woman who had a phenomenal tattoo. She told me she used a great artist in Santa Cruz, California. I went and saw her and showed her some of this stuff that I liked and that spoke to me. What impressed me about her was that she spent an hour with me just getting to know me and talking about what I liked about the pieces I showed her. For the caliber of artist that she was, I was very impressed with how collaborative it was. It wasn't like, 'This is *my* piece. What are you doing telling me about what you want to do?' Then she said, 'Okay, I'll try to create this one.' Her method was getting to know me and seeing some of the things I liked. She thought she could do something that I'd like.

At first she wrapped my leg with cellophane, and then she outlined where the tattoo was going to go so that when she wrapped it out flat she could sketch it. Then she did a sketch and I went back in and we looked at the sketch and I said, 'I really like this part, and I would change this part a little.'

I have a very high pain tolerance. I've done a root canal without any anesthesia. This hurt. This hurt especially right around the ankle and over my Achilles tendon where the skin is very thin and there's bone or tendon right below. I was pretty impressed with how much it hurt.

It was about two ten-hour sessions and one six-hour session. The ten-hour sessions were about two hours of doing the stencil laying. Then it was about two to two and a half hours of really painful needlework. Then after that, the numbing lotion was on, and it was less painful.

I think the final tattoo is a pretty good combination of something you'd see in Pacific Northwest and Native American patterns. At the top and the bottom, there's a bird-like image that spirals around my leg like a beak. What I really like about it is how it flows. It's got a lot of curves in it. She created this and I love it.

My sister-in-law said, 'Oh, man, did you have a midlife crisis or something?' My response was: 'Thank you for considering me in midlife.'

I've become surprisingly addicted to the idea of more tattoos. You can see the tattoo on my leg if I'm wearing shorts, but if I'm wearing pants nobody would know the difference. I like it enough that I'm definitely going to do something on my arm that's more visible most of the time.

29

OFF-COLOR HUMOR IN RETIREMENT: TESTING THE LIMITS

*"The kind of parties that we like to do are
to get people quietly uncomfortable."*

When you meet Tom, you immediately see his sense of humor. It's always been there, but maybe it's become more pronounced in his retirement.

One of his noteworthy accomplishments is being the creator of the Tacky Tavern Tour.

Tom's good humor pervades his activities with family, friends, and the community.

My wife and I run what we refer to as a Tacky Tavern Tour. You can have a group of up to six or eight people and we will take you to a minimum of five establishments somewhere in our county. At each one of these establishments we buy one beer, and at one of them we have a dinner. We more or less guarantee you these would be places that you've never been to and ones which, if you were on your own, you'd probably never go into.

They're the kind of places where about 80 percent of the women in the bar have a tattoo. Most of the people in the place have more fingers than teeth. In one place you might see a sign on the wall that says I BELIEVE IN GUN CONTROL; THAT MEANS HOLDING THE GUN WITH BOTH HANDS.

These places are off the beaten path. Many of them don't have a sign out front, other than some sort of cheap beer sign where half the neon isn't lit up anymore. When you go in, you might notice that whatever they have hanging on the wall hasn't seen a dust rag in probably ten or fifteen years. It's always kind of fun. What you find in there is that you've got regular real-life people who are fun to talk to. I don't mean to be making fun of anybody. We just like seeing what some of the other people who are out there are like. You get into all sorts of interesting discussions. Of course, nowadays if you do it, you find out their political leanings pretty quickly. If you're smart, you stay off that subject because you're likely to get shot.

My wife and I have to research this ahead of time. We go to all these places ahead of time and then we give them a little bit of fair warning that we're going to bring people by to visit them. Of course, the taverns love it because it's a little bit more business for them all.

One of our tours led us into a bar the other night in this little town of Wauconda. There was a guy playing pool there with a parrot on his shoulder. You don't see this every day of the week. Some of the people in our group egged me on into playing this guy in a game of pool. The only way he would play me is if I took the parrot and put it on my shoulder while we played, which I did. It was the first time I'd ever played pool with a freaking parrot on my shoulder. I was worried about whether the parrot was housebroken. And even with the worry of the parrot on my shoulder, I did win the game.

It's maybe sad to relate this, but a number of my wife's friends' husbands have either died or mysteriously disappeared. That leaves a lot of widows and divorcees as friends. Occasionally they like to get together for some social occasion. I end up with one or two other men plus eight women in a noisy restaurant. We make it significantly noisier by our presence. I think they relish having a male to talk with on occasion. It's very difficult having a conversation when there are six or seven of them talking at the same time. Although they seem to have a knack for it, I haven't developed that ability thus far.

I will tell you it's gotten a little bit easier. I had a great big seven-passenger SUV, which I purposely traded in for a five-passenger SUV, so now there can only be four I'm driving around at any one time. It makes life a little bit quieter. I purposely didn't get the heated seats in the back seat, just because I didn't want them to feel too comfortable.

Let me tell you about the volunteering aspect of retirement that I enjoy. One of the jobs I do is driving old people to doctor's appointments for a group called Elder Care. I'll get a call that somebody needs to go to a doctor at a certain time in three or four days, and then I wait for them to be done and then I drive them home.

The neat part of it is that you meet some relatively interesting people. Just to get them going (if I haven't met them before), I will ask them to give me their life story in five minutes. It's typically fifteen minutes, but it's always a lot of fun. You learn a lot of new stuff and you find out all sorts of things about people.

There's a gentleman my wife and I both used to drive, who was eighty-seven years old. One day I was driving him to a doctor's appointment. On the way, he suddenly said, 'Tom, I decided to take up smoking.' I said, 'You may want to run that by your doctor when you're there.' He said, 'Oh no, I know what he's going to say. He'll say, 'Hell, you're eighty-seven, how bad could it be?' He proceeded to take up smoking.

The nice thing about volunteering: it's not as altruistic as it sounds. You end up meeting some of the nicest people who appreciate what you're doing for them. It makes you feel good while you do it. That's kind of fun.

I would describe my retirement as about 98 percent wonderful. I retired just about nine years ago. I really never worried about what I was going to do in retirement. In my case, it's wondering how I can get more crammed into a day. I just have a gazillion hobbies that I like to do. I never had time to do them when I was working, or never had time to do them as much as I wanted. In that regard, the 98 percent is just the freedom to kind of play it as it comes, do things you like to do, but do a little bit more of that.

There are a whole bunch of advantages of having a little bit more time at your discretion. I enjoy reading a local newspaper in the morning, spending more time outdoors, and planting stuff in the garden. I read a lot more books now. The whole idea of setting up places to go and planning trips is fun. There's enjoyment in all of this.

The disadvantages are you're getting old. You're forgetting stuff. You don't know why you walked into that room. You have friends who are dying. You've got those things to deal with. I find it interesting and sometimes frustrating that everything I do takes longer to do. You don't have the deadlines that you had when you were working. You get in the middle of something—then you get distracted into something else. You go and do that. Forget. You come back to it. Everything takes like three times longer.

I like it 98 percent. The 2 percent of things I don't are things like the parrot. It's pretty hard for me to have a meal without slopping something down the front of my shirt. Not that I'd throw the shirt away. No, I'll throw it to the laundry in hopes that the stain comes out, and if it does not, use it as a painting shirt.

In retirement, you're old, and that's one of the things that just happens. For some reason, the older you get, the more crap falls off your spoon as you eat, and it typically goes down your shirt. I get to order what I want to order, but friends are constantly watching me. I think they take bets on how long it's going to take. Then they celebrate when that little blob of the chocolate that was in the ice cream just drops down on my shirt. It's just the way it works, but that's one of the issues that you do face in retirement. You've got to get used to it. But hey, if that's the worst of it, how bad could it be?

The shirt I have on today, it looks like there are just a few drops of some kind of a soup that's on it, but you've got to be standing pretty close to me to see it. That was an old dribble. I haven't had lunch yet today, so there's undoubtedly going to be some company there, but that's the way it goes.

Most of the people I hang out with, their eyesight's not so good anyway. It's not going to show up.

30

SURFING AND AGING: A RECONCILIATION

"Even when you're out there surfing for just two hours, you've got this glow all night long."

Bill has been a world-class surfer for all of his life. Surfing is his passion. Retirement satisfaction means being able to continue as an active surfer. As he watches his fellow surfers age, he has seen how they adjust to a body that is getting older. He has learned from their example. The pension and health benefits from his union job as a carpenter allow him the financial flexibility to continue to surf.

The union helped me over the years because of the benefits. You got a pension and you got a health plan. That's the key thing, and the wages are pretty good. When I was young, I was smart enough to know that the union was a good thing. Now that I've retired, it's like a huge, huge difference.

When I go surfing now, I try to do stretches and exercises. The main thing is your take-off. You can't stand up fast enough. Your back and shoulders and your hips just aren't quick enough and flexible enough to hit your feet that fast. Surfing is really the best conditioning, but you should do cross-training as well. The best professionals all have trainers, so they train all of these other muscle groups so they don't get out of balance.

When you're retired, you find your age is limiting it a little bit. A few older people gave me a heads-up that my energy level is going to be lower. I'm going to get tired faster, and my flexibility and prowess will decline a little. I have to stay active in order to not decline. I'm still just trying to stay on my surfing. A lot of my friends are drifting out of it as it becomes more difficult. They get frustrated and quit.

The amount of surfing that I do still depends on the weather. It could be no days during the week or it could be up to six or seven days a week. It'll just go through little cycles. Right now, I've been having a great time for the last six weeks because it's been really good to surf.

It's always a big thrill to surf the big waves. Even when you're out there for just two hours, you've got this glow all night long in your body and your mind. You can still feel it for hours and hours and hours.

Everything seems like life and death most of the time. One time I almost drowned out there. The dog was in my car. When you're almost drowning, all these things flash in your mind. Of all things, all I could think about was my dog in the car by himself. I finally grabbed the surfboard leash in one hand and got to the surface that way. You can come up and you've just barely survived. You're way out of breath. You've got to get some good breaths before another wave comes.

I try to do other things too, like walking. Even when I windsurf, those are completely different muscles. I'm still standing on a board, so it's like riding the wave. The difference is no paddling, and hanging on to the sail.

31

STUNNING ADVENTURES: SEEING THE WORLD

"We're going to go somewhere and we're going to travel."

> Nancy and her husband have a busy retirement, traveling to exotic places and then being active in the community when they return.

I never pictured myself this age. We're having a great time. We travel a lot. We've always wanted to do that and never did much of it. When our kids were growing up, we had a house up at Bear Valley in the mountains, so that was where we went. Now we are free to go all over.

We kept saying, 'We're going to go somewhere and we're going to travel,' and then say, 'Why are we going there?' Because we can. We want to do it while we can. We've been to so many different wonderful places. My favorite was down in South Africa in a park that abutted Kruger National Park. I almost cry when I think about it. The first night we went out on a game drive. The guide said, 'See this dead warthog ahead? I bet a young leopard killed it.' The next morning, we went out again and the warthog was gone, so we had to find the leopard. We found the leopard in a tree and the warthog was with him. The leopard ended up being like a kid to us all. We had to go back twice a day and see what he was doing. The warthog was gone by the end of the five days. The last time we saw the leopard, he was in the tree and there was a herd of hyenas below him and they were hissing at him. It was like a catfight then. It was so memorable because it seemed like we'd adopted this leopard and he was ours.

When we traveled to Vietnam, we had the most amazing guide. Once, he stopped the bus near a field of green onions. He got us all off the bus. He introduced us to this lady working the onion field, who he didn't know, and she told us all about her life. It was a unique thing to do. Another time, we were driving through a town and he said, 'There's a lot going on in this town today. I think there's a wedding. Let's stop the bus and go to the wedding.' Those of us who'd had daughters get married knew, you don't just drop in on a wedding with this tour group. We went to this wedding and sat in on it all, and learned the customs. One of them had to come down the stairs, and if he didn't, that meant the wedding was off. Was he going to come or was he not going to come? People were sitting around a big table and the couple came down. They must have exchanged some vows, but we didn't speak Vietnamese, so we didn't know what they did.

I just have one kid I tutor. I've tutored her since she was in fourth grade, and now she's going to be a freshman in high school. She's become like a grandchild. I've always enjoyed working with kids. It's a little girl who needs a lot of help in math.

She's become a leader in the class, which she had never been before. The kids awarded her this award for outstanding student in the class. That was really nice to see. I think success in school has given her a lot more confidence in herself.

I just like to help people. I think that's been something I've liked all my life.

I'm also the President of the homeowner's association. It's nice that I have the time to do it. The residents are either retired or semi-retired or this is the first home they've bought. We've been part of a couple of different homeowner's associations, so I had some background in how they run and what you should do.

Right now, we're in the middle of a binding arbitration with our builder over construction defects. That's scary. But the association also does fun things. We have a lot of international people here, and for our party, everyone brings a dish from their culture.

The young people help you know what's going on. One of the girls across the street works for Google and the other's a researcher at Stanford. They're so interesting. We had them over here on Sunday night. They're nice. They're interesting. They know new things.

32

A POETRY COURSE WITH EIGHTEEN-YEAR-OLDS: EXERCISING THE BRAIN

"Taking a poetry course is going to force me out of my comfort zone."

> In his retirement, Mike has picked up the pace of taking care of himself. He tests his limits by keeping active and trying new things, both physical and mental.

Retirement has given me a huge sense of relief. It's true. There was a song that was put out by Bob Seger. In it, there was a line where he sang, 'deadlines and commitments.' Since I've retired, I don't worry about deadlines and commitments like I did.

I'm having more fun now than I've ever had. I was not one who really couldn't wait to get to work every day. I still found other things more compelling. I'm doing lots and lots of things now, which time allows me to do, focusing on developing the body and the brain.

I do lots of physical fitness things like bike riding, spinning, tennis, golf. I do all kinds of different things. My favorite is all-day hiking.

I also found that I'm able to develop some social relationships that I have not had time for in the past. I can be available if somebody wants me to come over and help them.

I'm taking an English class at West Valley College starting in January. It's creative writing. I'm going to be writing short stories and poems and that sort of thing with the eighteen-year-olds.

One of the things that you fear in retirement is becoming stagnant and not exercising your brain. I think by doing this, it's going to force me out of my comfort zone and get more intellectual things going on. I've always had an interest in poetry. I find that I have a creative mind. I can handle words. I have dabbled in poetry, but never seriously. I have some things that I've accumulated over the years, so I can cheat. If the instructor gives me an assignment, I could go grab something and hand it in. But I would prefer keeping the brain working on new things. Some of what I'm interested in is just the feedback on what I do. If I had the instructor's attention and he or she found something that's pretty interesting, it might open new paths to do some things that I would enjoy. There may be other retired guys deciding to do the same kind of thing, and that would be fun. Then I'd get to meet some new people.

Feedback will be coming from both my peer group and instructor. That will be fun too. I fear that—especially at my age—I'm going to be a little didactic with my classmates. 'This is the way you're supposed to do it *because I* know.' Being in a room of eighteen-year-olds is likely to be very stimulating. I'm thinking it's going to help me understand younger generations. I'll be observing them and annoying them. They used to call all the people who were retired going back to classes DAWs, the Damn Average Wreckers.

I had an extra incentive because I just had bilateral knee surgery. Starting this class, I knew I wasn't going to be doing significant traveling during this time, so I'd be more available to attend the classes. I might have done it anyway, but I think that was part of the decision to take the class.

Dedicating yourself to improvement in retirement is really important. What I've tried to do is be physically active, socially active, mentally active—working all the puzzles.

33

FLY FISHING INTELLECTUALISM: A HOBBY ADDICTION

"Fly fishing is an intellectual challenge."

> **Rich retired at age fifty-eight so that he would have at least ten good years of retirement. His fly fishing has become an important part of his retirement years.**

I fly fish. I'm addicted to fly fishing. For years, my wife kept saying, 'We have to take up fly fishing.' Now I think that the real reason she said that was because of the movie *A River Runs Through It*. She was hoping she'd meet Brad Pitt on the river.

Fly fishing is complicated. To start out, you really do need a two-and-a-half-day course. Our teacher was the same guy who taught Tom Brokaw. This guy was just incredible. After that, we started fly fishing. We just became more and more excited about it and actually addicted to it. The reason you become addicted to this is, believe it or not, fly fishing is an intellectual challenge. You have to be an entomologist. You have to know all about the aquatic insects. You're constantly learning things and constantly studying and progressing from merely fishing to actually tying flies. You never step in the same river twice. It's always different. You're always in a beautiful place. And if you're always in a beautiful place, you can't lose.

Some days the fish win. The fisherman doesn't win every day. Other days you win and that's what brings you back. That is what gets so many people addicted to fly fishing. It's a lot of fun to look out on a river, on a flat pool, and suddenly see bugs coming up. Then you see the concentric circles and the dimpling in the river of the fish coming up to take the bug off the surface. You try to figure out what bug it is. You tie it onto your line, you throw it out there, and by golly, a fish comes up and takes your fly. Almost all fly fishermen throw everything back. It's catch and release. It's about the process of how you catch it.

Where we are located, I can be fishing on the Yellowstone in five minutes. In a half hour I can be in the park fishing the park rivers. In a couple of hours I can be over at Henry's Fork. I tell people that you will get bored of fishing any river. You need more than one river to fish. Even if it's a great river, you're eventually going to get tired of going to that same river every day. You want to be around a lot of rivers, and it's best to be around a lot of great rivers.

I fish basically every day. Initially, I just could not comprehend how anybody could possibly want to go fishing every day. But that's what I do. If you do it, if you're a fly fisherman, it's addictive. You can certainly understand why you'd want to go fly fishing every day. You might think, what about the grizzly bears? What about rattlesnakes? The thing is that you can't hunt for grizzly bears or rattlesnakes and fly fish at the same time. You can only do one and not both. You ignore those other risks and you focus on fishing. I can't tell you how many times I've been so intent on fishing that I almost walked into a buffalo in the Yellowstone National Park. You do have to look out for buffalo, wolves, and grizzly bears, but it's hard to do. You try to think about other things. You try to stop and take in the scenery, which I always do. It's always beautiful, but it's not as easy as you might think. I know that's hard to understand if you don't fly fish. How can you be out there for maybe eight hours a day and not do much else?

Henry David Thoreau once said, 'Most men fish all their lives and they never realize it's not the fish that they're after.' There's a lot of truth to that.

34

DEFYING PHYSICAL LIMITS: FINISHING HIS NINETEENTH MARATHON

"I definitely have embraced doing what I can't."

Don is seventy-six and retired from his insurance career ten years ago. His intensity and competitiveness are immediately apparent. His retirement gave him time to train even more intensely as he approached his nineteenth marathon.

Number 19 was different. His body gave him cues while he was running. He knew he was nearing his limit. He got support from one of his fellow runners, and his wife and a supportive group who were at the finish line.

After his nineteenth, Don had to consider how to adjust his training routine so he could run his twentieth marathon, which was scheduled in the next few months.

'm going to sound like I'm just bringing up the good things, because this stage of my life was scary to me. Am I really in my seventies? I'm going on beyond that and looking forward to the next adventure. I can embrace my age, and I feel grateful to have made it through all this time. It's an attitude you have to adopt—a lot of people don't get to this point. To be so blessed is to be able to look and do what I want to do. The things I want to do are very aggressive because I'm a guy that's competitive. I want to be challenged. I compete with myself. I love it.

I definitely have embraced doing what I can't. If I ever said to myself, 'I can never do that,' I'd say, 'Really? Really?' In my mind, there's nothing different now. As a matter of fact, I've never ever reached the point physically where I feel like I'm not doing just as well.

We've been blessed enough and lucky enough to be able to go to Maui. I ran the marathon out there. It's a hot place. Dehydration was a worry. I had to say, 'I'm pulling back. I'm going to pace myself. Try to be smart. Pacing yourself is very important in the marathon.'

It made me laugh. I said to myself, 'Are you kidding me? Can I be doing this? Really?' It was the biggest thing I've worked on recently. I can do this Maui Marathon. I've been wanting to run the Maui Marathon.

I was going at a good pace. I paced it out well, I think. The first thirteen miles took about two and a half hours. That way it was a five-hour marathon. That was fine. In the second half of that marathon, the gloves were off. What was going to happen next? I went around the next corner. I'd been going fine and all of a sudden all heck broke loose. What was happening? It was a different thing. I pulled back. I felt like I was running fast. It felt no different. I looked at my watch and said, 'Shit, Jesus, man, I'm hardly moving, what's going on?'

The emotion was so much. Could I think it through? During a marathon, you're always thinking *How am I doing? Okay. Come on, let's pull back a little bit. Wait a minute, I think I can go now a little bit.* You really think. Marathons are a bit mental, a bit physical, and trying to get both of those things in sync.

People were so wonderful. Good people. This one lady named Jennifer came up to me with a mile and a half left, and she said she was having trouble too. She said, 'We're going to do this together.' I said, 'You've got to be kidding. That's very sweet.' She was talking me through it. I was just trying to tell myself that I'm pushing it and crossing that line. Maybe I was doing something stupid, but when it came down to it, I couldn't wave the flag. I'm glad I didn't. I had to finish that sucker or I was going to be flat on my face. People will be saying, 'There's a guy out there who's crawling. His hands are bleeding.' I blocked that out and I just couldn't stop. Then I hit the last mile. That was when I thought I could do it.

I had about thirty yards to go and I said to Jennifer, who was still with me, 'Is that the finish line? Really, is this finished?' There were groups of people there waiting for people to come in. They just like to do that. I once again stopped. I couldn't move. I looked at these people, and they had horror on their faces. They were looking at me. Oh my God. My legs were locking and I was just trying to get so I wouldn't fall. Then sure enough, I could move again. I was moving. It was just quite amazing. These people started cheering. It was so emotional that I got embarrassed. Then they were cheering and I was moving and I couldn't believe these people. They were saying, 'Nice going, man. Nice going. Nice going.' It was amazing.

Then I got to the end. I was hardly moving, but the people were so warm. It was almost surreal. I've been there before and I've helped people, but I always had it in the back of my mind that they just didn't quite train enough. I trained. I trained. Look at me. You're a freaking mess, man. Then they cheered as I went by. I crossed the line, and then I was getting sick. Then somebody said, 'You need an IV.' My wife was on the finish line and I was lying there. I looked at her, and I was getting sicker and sicker. This was a new experience. Scary. Scary. I said to her, 'I don't know. I don't know. I'm not ready to try to jump up, hug and give you a kiss goodbye. I don't know, you better hang here.' Then I went in and I got sick. I had an IV and the IV was beautiful. It was fifteen to twenty minutes later and that pain was pretty much under control. The nurses and a couple of doctors pulled me out of this. I don't think I was in any horrible risk. I really don't, but I'm not sure.

I know it was temperature- and humidity-related, and that's what I'm trying to work on. I've got to get back in the saddle. I've got the California International Marathon coming up in less than a month. It's in Sacramento. You jump right back on the horse. Horse, here we go again. You do what you can.

I feel good. My legs are very tired. The recovery thing: I don't have it straight. I don't know what to do. I'm going to run a few maintenance runs, but I say I'm done running long. I'd better err on the side of recovering first. I do want to enjoy this. I do want to have fun, and I do want it to be a good experience.

My training routine changes because I don't know what to do with the recovery. I used to be able to go out at a certain time, and go like eight miles. Then go out twelve miles in two or three days. I didn't see it coming. The recovery, I don't know what the heck I'm doing. I've never known, because I'm always reaching, always reaching. I don't have the answers, especially the older I get. I thought I'd have it figured a little bit better by now.

If I'm more efficient with the marathon, I want to do a better job. That's why the California International Marathon is important. That's why the twentieth marathon is important. I want to get it. It's a good time for me even though old age scares me. It scares me. We're getting older. I'm grateful for every day. I've been swinging and grabbing at things and saying, 'Okay, this is good. We're putting all this together.' That's been the story of my life. I feel like I've been guided through this.

I've always believed there was more beyond our life. I've got to believe that because otherwise I could not make it. I don't think I could be as good a person when I considered doing good things if I didn't believe it. It feels like there's got to be something more than that. I've developed a standpoint that I want to grow. I want to learn. It's been a central part of my life.

My religious part changed dramatically for me when my latest dog was dying. My dog Lucy was an important part of my life. I just dropped on my knees one time and said, 'God, I can't handle this. I don't know when to put Lucy down. I don't want her to have pain. What am I supposed to do?'

Anyway, that worked out and I promised that I would be open to learning new things and answering my questions about belief. It's become a big part of my life. Just learning. I'm not a religious person, but I *am* a religious person. I believe in things out there because I couldn't function alone right now if I didn't feel like I've been growing every step of the way. It is a big part of my life and I'm sharing it with my family as much as I can. This is what helps me in my life. This is where I dig down when I'm having trouble and looking for guidance. Just guidance. What am I supposed to be doing now? Overall, I think it might have made me a better person.

GIVING BACK: MAKING SOCIAL IMPACT

I n his recent book, aptly called *The Second Mountain,* New York Times columnist and author David Brooks describes how your career is the first mountain. He then asks: What is your second mountain? What can you do now that will build on your current skills and make a difference in your community, and is something that you will enjoy doing?

The stories in this section give examples of people climbing their second mountain. They tell about their experiences of volunteering and provide snapshots of several different types of volunteer activities.

The path to finding the right volunteer opportunity is not covered in the interviews. This introductory section gives a bit more of the "how to" questions that each of these people have asked themselves. The questions below will provide the right path to a volunteer activity for you. The list is a compilation of wisdom from multiple interviews.

1. Is volunteering right for you? All of the people in the following stories came to the conclusion that they wanted to volunteer somewhere in this stage of their lives. But other interviewees in other sections of this book came to the opposite conclusion and decided to fill this stage of their lives with non-volunteering activities. There is a path to a joyful retirement either with or without volunteering. It's up to the individual to do a bit of introspection and decide if volunteering is a category of activity to consider.

2. What are some causes that you care about? You may feel passionate about climate change, or you may want to help one of your neighbors get to their doctor appointment. The range of causes is huge, but finding one that appeals to you takes some thought.

3. What type of organization appeals to you? Large or small? Local, national, or international? Perhaps you don't wish to be part of any organization at all and would rather volunteer your time via solo efforts.

4. Do you prefer hands-on, or mentoring, or something managerial? You can be the person who does physical things, like cooking or serving in a soup kitchen or putting away books in a library. You can guide others and teach them new skills so that they can become more effective. You may consider a leadership or governance role in which you guide a whole project, including the work of others.

5. What flexibility do you need to allow volunteering to fit with the other activities of the rest of your life? You need to figure out about how much time you are willing to contribute. You are a volunteer and not an employee. You have earned the right to insist on your flexibility to take a vacation or to miss a week of volunteer duty. The important point at the outset is to figure this out and communicate with the organization so that you're on the same page. The organization, from its perspective, is entitled to know what they routinely can and cannot expect from you. Do what you say you will do, and if you do more, that is a bonus to the organization.

6. Are your skills applicable? Potential volunteers worry way too much about this one. Yes, you are almost certainly qualified. You are not going to be a volunteer brain surgeon. You are going to be someone who pitches in and helps in whatever

way makes the most sense for you and the organization. Many organizations have perfected the art of matching their objectives to your interests and capabilities, and you will see that in some of the stories that follow.

7. How do you find your specific volunteer opportunity? Most of the volunteering discussed in this section is the result of networking conversations with friends and family. Make it known that you are on the prowl looking for a volunteer opportunity, and give as much definition as you can about what sort of activity you are seeking. Like all good networking, when you talk to someone about the subject of volunteering, your last two questions should always be "Who else should I talk to?" and "Will you give me an introduction?" There is also an internet way to find interesting opportunities. A place to start is at www.volunteermatch.org. You can put in your search criteria, including your location, and it will produce a list of possibilities to consider.

8. Can you try it and see? Yes, absolutely! A starting assumption may be that you will do some trial and error. If you like it, stick around. If you don't, it's time to move on. What does not work for you is also not working for the organization. Be clear at the outset that you want to try the activity for a while to see if it is right for you. The stories that follow are the results of a trial-and-error process to find the right volunteer opportunity.

As you read the stories in this section, you will begin to appreciate what it's like to be a volunteer in each of the settings that are described. You will get a sense of what the retiree gets from that experience. Giving back and having social impact is part of the motivation. Camaraderie, learning new skills, and meeting new people can all add to the richness of the volunteering opportunity. Although there are several different types of volunteering shown in these stories, they only scratch the surface of the wide range of possibilities to consider.

35

A NATURAL TRANSITION: FROM BANKING TO NONPROFIT

"There's not much more that we can do that's more emotional than giving a family the keys to their house that they have helped build."

Larry did not skip a beat during his transition to retirement. He'd had a career in banking and had developed his managerial, leadership, and governance skills. He had dabbled in volunteer work for Habitat for Humanity. Once he retired, he was able to immerse himself in addressing the affordable housing shortage and fully adapt his existing skills to a new task.

My life now is both fun and interesting. My primary job—I will call it work, or volunteering, or avocation, whatever it is—is with Habitat for Humanity. That's just incredibly rewarding. It sometimes feels like I'm just involved in a successful business enterprise, but it happens to be a nonprofit doing great things.

What I did as a banker was interesting and can be very helpful in this organization, but I've learned a whole lot more in a nonprofit. There's no stagnation at all because the challenges we face are different, because of what we do. The environment is so ever-changing. Working in housing and housing development, the need is so incredibly great.

Housing is on many people's list as one of the top two or three problems that we face as a region. What's important and enjoyable about what we're doing is that Habitat started out just building houses—that was all we did. But things have evolved, and we've been one of the leaders within the Habitat community around the country to really branch out and find additional solutions to the housing problem. There isn't a single solution. Things like a counseling operation, doing repairs for low-income seniors who have been in their homes for a long time and can't afford necessary repairs, work on manufactured housing, building sleeping cabins for the homeless, as well as participating in housing projects internationally.

There are roles and opportunities, regardless of what your background is, because we need all different types of skills and perspectives. We want to reflect the communities we live and work in. We need people who will provide that kind of perspective. We don't need people who all bring exactly the same thing to the table.

Habitat is organized through affiliates. There is a parent organization, Habitat for Humanity International. Then there are locally run affiliates.

A neighbor of mine had just gone on the board. He said, 'The way Habitat works is we raise money. We build housing. The fundraising and the community involvement is done through organizations such as churches and civic groups, and a lot of corporate engagement and activity. I really think that a small community like ours, like Moraga, should be able to sponsor a house, provide the funding, and help build a house for a needy family. The house wouldn't necessarily be in our community. It would be wherever Habitat might be building or we might have available land.'

He said, 'So, I'm going to organize this. Do you want to be involved?' I said, 'Sure.' He started walking down the street and then he came back and said, 'By the way, I want you to co-chair this with me.' I said, 'Okay, well, let's do this. It could be fun.' We got started and, with some fits and starts, organized the community advisory board, raised money, and ultimately ended up sponsoring and helping to build a house in a Habitat development.

I've been on the board, the finance committee, all kinds of activities. For a good while also, I was out helping pound nails and build things. I'm not doing any nail pounding anymore. I actually messed up both my shoulders through building with Habitat. So now it's all board, committees, management kinds of things. I chair a subsidiary that we formed two or three years ago. I'm on the board of directors of the organization and on the finance committee forever. I'm really doing governance kinds of things as one would do in a typical for-profit company.

Habitat doesn't give houses away. We sell them. There's always a waiting list. We can't build nearly enough for the demand, especially in this area. Families have to be employed, have to have good credit. We have a counseling group that can help people improve their credit standing and teach them good financial management habits, et cetera. Then they put five hundred dollars equity into the construction of their homes. They then take on a mortgage at no interest. It's a heck of a different deal than a typical residential mortgage. Every penny they pay goes to pay down the loan they have.

There are three items presented at a Habitat dedication. One is a hammer that is a symbol of what we have done to help build their home. The second is a book of faith of their choice, whether it be a Bible or a Quran or whatever it might be. The third is a symbolic key. There's nothing that's more emotional than giving a family the keys to their house that you and they have helped build. You turn it over to them and wish them luck. You give them a hug and send them along to, hopefully, a whole lot of success as a family.

A number of our families are immigrants. There was one gentleman who received a house in the San Jose area. This gentleman was from an African nation and had been struggling to really help his family grow and succeed. He came in and there was a typical ceremony, where the homeowner might say something and we have a presentation of the keys. This man was so moved, he got down on his knees. He was crying and soon everybody started crying. He wrapped his arms around our board member who was presenting this symbolic key to him. He was just in tears. He was so overjoyed.

You watch this nice, strong, very hardworking gentleman. It was so incredibly emotional that it totally stopped him. There's not much you can say other than congratulations. He went to every person who was involved with Habitat who was there, and he was hugging and thanking. You realize this is a person who has strived so hard to get what he had. You knew he was going to take that opportunity and get great success out of it. There truly was not a dry eye in the house.

Four years ago, former President Jimmy Carter and Mrs. Carter visited with us in Oakland and in San Jose. For a Habitat facility to get selected for this, it's a heck of an honor because it means that you're doing something right. You also must have the capacity to do something really productive and use their time effectively. We were thrilled when we were given the opportunity. The impression I got from people who worked with him was that he was very serious and no-nonsense. His focus was 'Let's build, we're here for the mission.' He understood his role and was very gracious and helpful and interested. He was not there for show. He really did get down and actively work and build. Some people who would be in that kind of role might well just be there for the cameras and to make an impression.

One other anecdote struck me. As I was preparing to retire, I ran into a person who'd retired from where I worked. I asked him how he was doing and he said, 'I flunked retirement.' I said, 'How do you flunk retirement?' He said, 'I was so worried about not having enough to do that everything that came along I signed up for, because I was so worried about having not enough to do.' He said, 'I've got more to do than I did when I was working full time. I've got to figure out how to scale this back, because how do I give the right time to people where I really should be involved and can be really helpful?' He said, 'I flunked.'

36

MAINTAINING A LEGACY: A PRESCHOOL WITH A UNIQUE PHILOSOPHY

"I guess it's my dream of making sure that this school goes on. I have tried to put in place something to assure its future."

Jane was first involved with Mountain School forty years ago and has been a teacher and an administrator there since then. Just weeks ago, she retired from her day-to-day activities. She felt it was time to step aside and let others run the school operations. Jane's mission now is to identify challenges facing the school for the longer term and develop plans to make sure that the school is able to continue to provide its values-based education to preschoolers.

When she's not busy with the school, Jane and some girlfriends are learning to play the ukulele. They decided that their seventies was the right time.

This stage of my life is fairly new because I only retired officially in June. I don't know what is going to happen. My life is already pretty full, so I'm not sure that there's a real drop-off or if I'm looking for things to do. I've been involved in a preschool for many, many years. Nature and children are the two threads throughout my life. I grew up in Yosemite, so I was very much into the natural world. I've been able to continue that in my own life and in the work with children.

I feel like I've got some history with the school because our daughter went there, and now our daughter is a teacher. She assisted in Mountain School and then our granddaughter assisted in a summer school session. Then two years ago, our great-granddaughter was a student in the two-year-old class. We've really had four generations.

I think for me the uniqueness of the school is the outdoor education piece. There's this three-legged stool of nature, observations, and cooking. To me, those are the core tenets of the school. We think it's really important for children to have creek time and creek play.

Parent involvement includes having to come and do observations. By the end of the year, they have a journal of what it was like. I was first introduced to the school when my two-year-old enrolled. At the end of the year, I had a journal of what my daughter Lisa was like as a two-year-old, which was fabulous. When she had her own children and her daughter became two, I went back to read the earlier journal. It was so interesting. I saw shades of Lisa within the uniqueness of granddaughter Lily. It's a lovely thing.

It's very rewarding for me. Parents have said, 'It changed our lives, because our parenting style would have been so different.' I think that's what I love so much about the school. You get to work with children, which I love. You also get to work with parents, and the combination is really good. Most of the teachers would say that it wouldn't be enough just to have the children. All of the teachers we've had have come from within the school. They have been parents themselves. Most of our teachers are not credentialed. They have been parents and we watched them. We see that they have something to offer. Usually, we try to get them to assist and then we see how they do. Then will they step up? I think working with parents takes another set of skills. You can be great with kids but maybe not that great with parents. That's really important to do that.

My decision to retire was triggered by the realization that I should step aside so other people could really take my place. Because as long as I'm there, they'll say, 'Teacher Jane does it this way.' I've been involved in this school for over forty years. I thought maybe this was time just to back off. It was time to make room for others.

I guess it's my dream of making sure that this school goes on. It's been around since the mid-fifties. There are some challenges in this day and age with different parenting styles. I've been concerned about some things, so I have tried to put in place something to assure the future of the school. I've been working on this for probably five years. I started out looking at different sites, because we meet outdoors as well as indoors. There are some places that the parents don't want their kids to go to—the creek, for instance—so that becomes an issue. We're always looking for new places. We can't use this place or that place anymore. I was concerned, are we going to lose a place? Can we find another place?

What's come out is that it's more than just locations. In addition to the location, there are concerns about the staffing and the financial. Everything needs to be done in a way that retains the institutional memory based on a very unique philosophy. I stopped being just the person who was looking to find locations, to being one who's developing more of a strategic board. We've just put together a strategic board which is made up of alumni who have a great love for the school and an understanding of it.

We had our first meeting a couple of weeks ago. That's very exciting. I think I will be involved in that, and that's probably a monthly meeting.

One of my friends is just passionate about everybody having a lot of music in their lives. She plays ukulele. She suggested that we get together and play. It's something that I've never done. Twice a month, we meet here and play ukulele. This has been going on for a couple of years. There's usually about six of us. I know half a dozen chords, but you can sing an awful lot of songs with just a few chords. It's fun. We laugh a lot. We tell stories as well as playing songs.

We had this little routine. My husband one day woke up and started singing that song, 'Accentuate the Positive,' so he said, 'I bet your group could sing that.' This was very early on. We start every session with 'Accentuate the Positive' and we end every session with 'Please Don't Talk About Me When I'm Gone.' In between, we sing lots of old-type songs. We just have a lot of fun. We're all new at ukulele and we're not struggling at all. We just play.

Out of that came what we call the Aloha Band. A friend who does hula came and talked to the children about hula and introduced them to it. Five of us go and play all the Hawaiian songs. That's an offshoot.

It's an easy instrument to play. I played piano all my life, but ukulele is really good and it challenges the brain in different ways.

37

TOO HARD TO PASS UP: VOLUNTEERING AT THE AMERICA'S CUP

"You've got to find what making a living prevented you from doing. That's why the America's Cup course marshal appealed to me."

> William has a love of all things nautical. As he was nearing his decision to retire, the possibility of volunteering for the America's Cup became the ultimate deciding factor.

As the company that I was working for had grown, I was getting bored. When they said America's Cup was going to be here in San Francisco, I said, 'That might be a good opportunity to retire, if I can find something as the course marshal on the water all summer.'

I had worked on America's Cup in high school in Newport, Rhode Island. I went back there and helped out during the trials, hauling sails and hauling lines and doing other things. I was part of the support area for a while and it was fun.

I'd already got my small boat certification in 2012 from US Sailing, so I was already prepared to do it and I think I was building myself up to that.

A course marshal is a person who drives around in a small boat—a RIB, rigid inflatable boat. He's assigned a sector on the course to basically keep the spectator boats off the course.

Some days it was really tough because of the tide coming in. When the tide's coming in, the spectator boats between the Golden Gate Bridge and the course are being pushed onto the course. The course marshal has to keep going up to people and saying, 'You're too far in, you need to be between point A and point B.'

Being that close to the fastest sailboats on earth was fabulous. I was out there this one day that there was an almost-collision between the two boats. I suddenly heard this big scream and I looked and saw the near miss.

The Oracle team was down, and they'd lost eight races out of the nine. They had a powwow on the water off Crissy Field. They called a whole bunch of the course marshal boats to surround them and keep the press boats and everybody else away, while they had to really decide what they were going to do. The Oracle team ended up making an amazing comeback. All of a sudden, they had figured out where the 'go' button was on that boat. They were really moving. It was the greatest sports comeback I've ever seen in any sport. It was even better than the baseball Giants parlaying a wild card into a win in the World Series.

It was just so much fun being out on that water, and being right in the middle of the action. That's why I retired, because my previous experience showed how close to the action you can get.

38

MOTIVATION TO HELP CANCER PATIENTS: YOUR OWN CANCER DIAGNOSIS

"We desperately need a caring house, where people taking cancer treatments here can have a place to stay."

Being diagnosed with prostate cancer was a springboard for Ag to take on the fight against cancer. He found new meaning in his retirement life by taking a leadership role in a project to support cancer care in his community. That fight led him to start helping other cancer patients in his Colorado community through personal support and counseling.

Ag and his wife have a variety of intellectual and cultural activities in both Austin and Colorado that provide additional richness to their retirement.

I f I'm going to describe my retirement, it's portrayed by David Brooks in his book *The Second Mountain*. I've been doing all kinds of things since I retired seventeen years ago, especially those personal activities that my career took me away from.

The second mountain means reevaluation of your goals and what you want to do. I spent my career just driving myself to be successful and to earn a substantial living. I really didn't have a lot of time for personal interests or looking out for other people. It was all my work.

I think the book perfectly describes the career focus in the first mountain. You dedicated all your time and energy to getting educated, having a lot of debt, getting that paid off, and building a career. As you move on in life, you realize that the rewards come also in other ways. Your interpersonal relationships with folks mean a lot more, and you spend more time focused on them. In these last seventeen years, I've thought more about doing things for other people.

A year before I retired, I was diagnosed with prostate cancer. Right after I retired, I had surgery and then had to have radiation. I did the radiation here in Colorado and got involved with the cancer center. I was halfway through my radiation treatment, working with a brilliant radiation oncologist. I asked her how I could help, fully expecting that she would seek a donation. She said, 'We desperately need a house where people taking cancer treatments can have a place to stay. They can't afford to stay in the valley. We need to build a caring house.' That took me on a journey that lasted six or seven years and has been really important to me.

It turned out there were six ladies already involved in trying to figure this out. There was a vice president of a local bank and folks from the entire spectrum of society, but everyone had this goal. I got involved with them. One thing led to another and we finally said, 'Well, we're going to have to raise about $5 million. We're going to have to get the land. We're going to have to get approvals. We're going to have to go to the board.'

I said, 'This is too much for a volunteer group. You need to hire an executive director.' They said, 'That's a great idea. I think we should.'

I went back to Austin for the fall and realized on the way home that maybe *I* should be that executive director. I applied for it and said that they had to pay me. I wasn't going to volunteer for it, because people wouldn't respect the guidance and the outcome unless it was a paid position. I said, 'I'll do it for half price.' They hired me.

I can remember when we did the first presentation for this house. The county commissioners turned us down and kicked it down the road. We were just ticked. We went to a local bar and drank beer for about two hours. We put the thing back together again and went back. We weren't going away.

The seven of us spent two years getting the approvals, going to local government, and we got the hospital to donate the land. I think they all thought we were a little crazy.

Then we spent another two years with our goal to raise $4 million. I think fundraising is about your attitude. I tried not to look at it like it was arm-twisting. I looked upon it as this great project that's going to not only help the cancer center become better known, but provide a wonderful service for people in our valley. All I'm doing is asking if you'd like to support it.

We had training sessions, and it was just a lot of laughs. Everybody loved it. Training these people was fun. We had such a good rapport that people would say, 'Well, I can't go up and ask somebody for $50,000.' I said, 'You're not going to ask them for $50,000. Ask them for $100,000 and then maybe we'll get $50,000.' That's what happened. People just couldn't believe it.

Before we made our first ask, we had one very generous gift of $1 million in the bank. This was set up in a trust to help pay the operating costs and the maintenance of this facility. We had a lot of fun doing it and the project had great success. We raised almost $5 million in about six months. The whole thing was oversubscribed. These people have never done that before.

I fired myself once we raised all the funds, and then became the project manager for the building of the house. I did that on a volunteer basis.

The caring house has been very successful. It's going strong. We just had our tenth anniversary. This was a great project. It's probably running at 80 percent occupancy today.

As it turned out, the project was a great springboard for me after saying, 'Hey, I don't want to work in corporate America anymore.' This wasn't stress. This was so enjoyable. We had a goal. It was wonderful. We were doing something and it was successful. It would emotionally pay off a thousand times over. With this kind of activity, you're rewarded as much or more as the person you're trying to help.

Reflecting on it, I think my diagnosis of cancer had a lot to do with it. At the time, when you're told that you have cancer, you know what the risks are. You analyze it and you can make decisions on your treatment plan. I think my decisions were correct, because I've been cancer-free for seventeen years. That's very emotional.

My cancer recovery and getting involved in the clinic was unbelievably gratifying. It's certainly a story that I'm just deeply proud of. I feel great and very positive. I feel like I really had a more complete life because of it. I think so many people get to the end of the road of a business career and they walk out the door and it's like falling off a cliff.

During this time, I also became a resource for the docs at the clinic. Some guys were having trouble dealing with their prostate cancer. I never had any training in it. I was able to talk to people about these sensitive issues. Men with prostate cancer can really face up to a 40 percent chance of being impotent for the rest of their life. That's a really hard one. You have people who first decide they're not doing the treatment. That's a very common response. You say to those guys, 'Well, do a time-out. How long do you want to live?

Two or three years, or twenty? There is a lot of fun in life after this stuff. If you don't have a plan, you're not going to be successful at it. It's that simple.' I was able to do that probably half a dozen times. It helps some people cross the bridge.

Late in my working career, we moved to Austin. We decided that we would put some roots down there and it became obvious that that's where we were probably going to retire. Austin today is a vibrant young city. The average age is thirty-four. Austin is a perfect balance of just about anything you might want to do. It's outdoors. It's in the hill country with rolling hills and lakes. I can go out my back door and ride my bike for twenty-five miles on trails within the city.

We now have a townhome that's five minutes from all the action. All the great restaurants and all the activities. The whole thing just works and we love it. It's great. The university really has some great things. One is the LBJ Presidential Library. They run a lecture series for about eight months of the year at the Lyndon B. Johnson School of Public Affairs. They have absolutely Class A speakers. That's wonderful and that's the benefit of a large college town. The university also runs what we call 'University for Old People.' For example, you study Iran for six weeks. Every Monday you get a two-hour lecture on it and stuff to read. We've been doing that for fifteen years. It's an intellectual draw that appeals to me. It gets your brain working in a little different direction. I think that's really important in retirement.

You've got to understand that around June 20 in Austin, it's going to hit 100 degrees, and you're going to get about fifty days of those between then and the middle of September.

One of our dreams had always been to have a place in the mountains in Colorado. We love the skiing and the outdoors. It ended up to be a perfect combination with Austin. It's nice from a weather perspective, and to have that break in Colorado for a couple of months is perfect.

There are things I like to do that I'm still able to do physically. We both like to ski. We're not doing it eight hours a day, but we probably go out for a couple of hours every morning. I like bike riding, which we do in the summer, and we take bike trips. That's a whole new activity that I discovered and learned how to do in my retirement.

The people here in the community are extremely generous. As a result, we have a classical music festival from the last week in June to the first week in August called Bravo, which these folks support. The first two weeks we have the Dallas Symphony in residence, the second two weeks we have the Philadelphia Orchestra in residence, and the last two weeks is the New York Philharmonic. We probably hit three-quarters of the performances, so we see sixteen or eighteen performances of world-class orchestras and guest artists.

My wife and I both work at achieving a balance of our activities. The body ultimately declines. If you've got a great mind going for you, it really helps the physical as well. We're all going to get hit with something. I'm very thankful to be where I am. I think that balance is really important.

39

LEAVING THE CORPORATE WORLD EARLY: APPLYING LESSONS LEARNED

"I think the fact that I'm involved in helping society in general is actually carrying a fair bit of weight with my kids. I think maybe one of the best benefits is what that says to our kids."

Peter is a reflective person. He continually questions himself about how to spend this stage of his life and how to find his elusive passion.

He retired from a Silicon Valley tech job when he was fifty-four. He identified a career trap: if you are good at something, you tend to keep doing it. He found a way to step out of that trap and try new activities.

For the last four years, he has found multiple unique roles in organizations that have a positive social impact.

I t took me a while to just be able to say, 'Yes, I'm good at this. But I don't really love it.' I didn't find that I burned for the work that I was doing. My wife and I agreed it was time to do something different.

I started interviewing for a different kind of high-tech job—both within my current company as well as outside. I was looking for something that would make me say, 'Okay, this is firing me up. *This* I'm excited about.'

The last two years of my job took a significant toll on me. I realized that I simply had no energy or desire to continue doing the kind of work I had done for the previous thirty years. I reached out to a place called Encore and did an Encore Fellowship. It was a very helpful transition from the highly intense structure of the corporate environment to a much less intense, but still structured, nonprofit environment. It had some emotional payback as well.

Encore is a nonprofit that was founded in San Francisco about twenty years ago. Its whole focus is on people who are baby boomers. Even though the average life expectancy for the American male is seventy-eight, it turns out that's a wildly misleading statistic. If you're fifty-five and in reasonably good health and with reasonable socioeconomic circumstances, you can expect to live to ninety. It's stunning. You can expect that you will have pretty good mental and physical abilities through most of that. If you're fifty-five, you can reasonably expect to have another twenty-five good years ahead of you. The idea of the golden years is an outdated one.

The concept of retirement was invented as recently as the 1950s and 1960s. We haven't caught up to the fact that we need a new term. We have childhood, we have adolescence, we have middle age, we have retirement, but we need a new name for the golden years. There are twenty-five years that are currently unaccounted for. Encore is really focused on changing the conversation around what people will do as they get older. One of the things that they do is the Encore Fellowship Network. You take people who are typically executives who are retiring from their companies and are interested in giving back to society in some way. They may not really know what that means. Encore acts like Match.com between executives and nonprofits. The Fellow goes in to work on some strategic project that is important for the nonprofit's growth but for which it has neither the resources nor the expertise.

The Fellow joins at half time for a year, for a $25,000 stipend, and essentially becomes a member of staff. There have been about two thousand of them so far in the last ten years. The nonprofit itself or a corporate sponsor pays the Fellow's stipend.

My Encore Fellowship was with an organization called Breakthrough Silicon Valley, and their focus is to help underserved middle school kids make it to a four-year college. The families are hugely enthusiastic backers, and that's a requirement. We don't ask the parents for anything, but they at least have to be supportive. Most parents are really excited for their kids. What I learned was that it's essential to bring some humility to the project. One of the biggest challenges is that so many executives come in like, 'Okay, we were paid to be decisive. We were paid to make decisions. We were paid to go, go, go.' Many nonprofits don't operate with that mentality. If you bring that go-go culture in, you're going to run headfirst into a brick wall. It's important to have the humility to realize that there's much that you don't know. You also have to tread carefully in sharing what you do know so that you can bring people along with you. If you can present your ideas in a way that's not patronizing and condescending, you can really have a substantial impact. There's almost always a 'come to Jesus' point about two or three months into the Fellowship where it seems like it just isn't working. It's really not working because the strategic project you were brought in to work on usually turns out not to be achievable. What you have to figure out is, how do we adjust so that I'm doing the things the organization *actually* needs rather than what they thought they needed.

When the Encore Fellowship was wrapping up, I had a conversation with our kids and said, 'Okay, so now what?' Their response was, 'What are you guys doing to the planet that we're going to inherit?' That's when the environmental thing came up. We're good Palo Altans. We do our recycling and I have an electric car. We have tried to model what's good behavior, but in a very easygoing way.

I wanted to do something a little bit more tangible that might actually help. I wanted to do more than just sitting around the table talking about the twenty terrible things that we're not really doing anything about.

I think climate change is just such a problem. You have a billion people in the world who don't have electricity. Finding ways to give people economic opportunity, lighting, and clean cooking seems like a moral imperative. And doing it in a way that doesn't make the climate crisis worse. It was a way to try and do something tangible about climate change.

The impetus to want to do something of more social value had been there for quite some time. Once my brain had thawed out a little bit, that was the place I went to. It was what I wanted to do. It was when I decided to join the Miller Center. The Miller Center runs a program called the Global Social Benefit Institute. It's run at Santa Clara University, a Jesuit university. Its goal is to take Silicon Valley entrepreneurial principles and use them to help social entrepreneurs throughout the world. Typically, a social entrepreneur applies to a program and they're paired up with two mentors who are usually Silicon Valley executive types. They work through a curriculum over the course of twelve to twenty weeks. Then it culminates usually in some sort of business plan or investor pitch.

I spend one day a week in there, helping in the energy access space. I've written a couple of mentor tutorials, including one on basic knowledge around the energy access sector. I think preparing tutorials has much higher scaling value. If I can help twenty mentors be somewhat more effective, that's a much better payback. That's always motivated me to find ways to help, one degree removed from the front line. If I help a kid become literate, that's great. I helped the kid. If I can help a program that helps hundreds of people help the kids, that feels better to do. There's not the same personal emotional investment. It's a little easier to write a manual. At the moment, I like the balance I have. I'm mentoring individual people. I still have that personal connection, which I think is good. At the same time, I feel I can be of more value by doing things that will help a larger number of people rather than just helping one person.

I think the fact that I'm involved in helping society in general is actually carrying a fair bit of weight with my kids. I think maybe one of the greatest benefits from what I'm doing is the message I'm sending our kids. This is something that they can do. I would talk a lot about what I was doing. That's a dinnertime conversation that we otherwise wouldn't have had. It's just a chance to talk about things that we would never have talked about before. As I look at it, one of the things I think is cool for our kids is that they have seen two parents who have reinvented themselves.

I think there's something important for our kids to realize: that you go to college, you pick your career, you do stuff, but in your forties or fifties you can then do something different. I think that's probably a great message for the kids. I have tried to not harp on it, but I think it has been good for them to hear about some of the people I've been helping and just to realize that you can change and grow.

I don't know that I'll ever be at a point where I just say I'm comfortable, that I have it the way I want it. I think I'm just genetically wired to always be thinking about what needs to be different. However, for many of my fifty-eight years, that's been kind of a constant theme that runs through my head. I think part of me just always thinks that

I need to be doing something different or need to be doing something more. I've made some fairly dramatic transitions and some of them still really sit uncomfortably with me. Retiring at fifty-four still feels wrong to me. It feels on some level wildly self-indulgent and reckless. Walking away from that prime earning period in my life was A) brave B) stupid or C) all of the above. If you're going to do it, then do it. There's nothing worse than doing it and agonizing over it, because now you're in the worst of both worlds. You've lost the money and you don't have the benefits. If you're going to make a decision, be conscious of the consequences and embrace it. It's important not to be halfway between one thing and the other.

40

TEACHING BUDDHIST MEDITATION TO PRISONERS: JUST ONE PART OF A COUPLE'S ECLECTIC RETIREMENT

*"I think the best part about all of it is
learning about people's humanity."*

- Jill

*"I feel lucky to have found Buddhist meditation. I think
if it was only baseball, it would feel hollow."*

- Bruce

Bruce and Jill have been married for fifty-two years. They retired over seventeen years ago, when Bruce turned sixty. Both remain physically active into their seventies. Their commitment to family and friends is an important part of this stage of their life. But they also needed to serve; they needed to give back after having been given so much from their community.

Teaching Buddhist mindfulness created the opportunity to serve in several ways. They regularly teach a meditation class at a Buddhist meditation center. Once a week, they also teach mindfulness meditation to prisoners in a maximum-security prison.

The goal was not to find satisfaction. It was to serve and do something worthy.

Jill: I describe this stage of my life as things coming together. All the experience and all the wisdom just coalescing. It's also a time of great learning, especially about changing bodies and mind and heart. I love being active. Right now, I do swimming and hiking and yoga and weightlifting. I do something every day, but I try to balance it. It's not too intense. I would describe myself as having less of an overabundance of energy than I once did.

Bruce: I've been retired for over seventeen years. I've loved my retirement. I was a physician before I retired and I loved my work. I would have to say that it's a great time in my life. My body is acting up and falling apart like it's supposed to, but in general, it's a great time in my life. I love what I do and the way I'm spending my time.

Jill: I still teach as a volunteer at a nursery school. I love kids and I love being goofy with them. I can be a participant or an observer of their play in a silly way so that I don't direct it, but I can extend it in some way.

It's all centered on them and having them experience whatever they're experiencing fully. I have this image of helping them stretch their arms out further.

Bruce: My passion since I was a kid is softball. At seventy-seven, I'm still very involved in softball. I'm playing on a seventy-five-year-old tournament team, and we just won the Western Regional Championship in Sacramento. One of the things I really like about softball is that it brings together people from all different walks of life, all different races, all different religions, all different political points of view. You just know them as the softball player and teammates or adversary that they are. Some people you find a little jerky, and a lot of people you find just fine, and some people you like a lot.

I love softball and it gives me motivation to stay fit. Only thing getting in the way of it now is I think I need a hip replacement. I'm playing through the pain, but it's starting to be clear that I can't really play the way I want to. It's getting clear that I'm going to have surgery.

Jill: For a long time, we've been very involved in teaching at the Buddhist mindfulness meditation center. These are people who voluntarily come who want to learn something about meditation. Part of what helps me teach is telling stories. What's key to the stories is being very human and using your own experiences as a way to emphasize or explain or to humanize the student's experience.

Bruce: We started teaching those new to Buddhist meditation practice. We just liked having a fresh group—a group that came in without a lot of preconceived ideas of what they needed to do or how to do it.

Jill: It's a big part of Buddhist practice to contemplate, to understand that this life is really precious, and it's also fleeting. That everything is changing all the time, including you. Every day you are getting a little closer to the end. Accept it as part of nature. There's nothing you can point to that's born that doesn't die.

Bruce: Developing the right attitude toward meditation is really important. From my own experience as a pre-med, I had to really drive myself hard to memorize and get to where I needed to be. I brought that attitude to meditation and it doesn't work at all. It's got to be much more relaxed and non-striving. You have to put in the energy, but it has to be with the right attitude. We really like to teach those who are new to practice.

Another passion is that from the time I retired up until right now, my wife and I have taught a Buddhist form of meditation in Salinas Valley State Prison. We've been doing that for seventeen and a half years.

Jill: We volunteer one day a week. It's very mixed. It's not entirely for enjoyment. It's really a sense of service. The intention is to be there.

Bruce: It's a tough prison. It's a maximum-security prison level four. Within that prison, one of the places we serve is the yard. It's been an interesting experience to work with the men there and to see them as human beings. There are lots of people of color because of the inequities of our justice system and the poor conditions that people of color often come up through; poor schools, not enough to eat, et cetera. The abandonment, neglect, the abuse and all that.

Jill: It's a difficult population. It's also a forgotten population. People would like to just erase them. I like interacting with people I'd never interact with otherwise. Not only the men inside, but the people who work there. They're from so many walks of life that are very different from my usual interactions.

We're volunteer Buddhist chaplains. Sometimes they've read about our program. Sometimes they've experienced it in different prisons. Sometimes somebody they know has come to our program. Sometimes they come because they're bored. They want to get out of their cell.

Bruce: The inmates know we have a Buddhist program and they volunteer to come. When we first went there, there were religious programs and Narcotics Anonymous and Alcoholics Anonymous.

There was a teacher who was teaching creative writing as well. There were very few self-help programs. We were the closest to a self-help program, so we had really big groups. We had twenty-five to thirty people, which actually makes it hard to teach. We were happy to have them, because they were learning. Now it's twenty at the very most, but more often five to ten.

Jill: There are days where it just doesn't feel like anything much is going on. It's different every day. You're not going there so that you can feel good. That is not the purpose of it. The intention is to show up and be a human being with them. Sometimes it's frustrating. I used to say if you have one good day out of four, it's pretty good. But we keep going back. Part of that is because we have a wonderful support group with the other people who volunteer. That's incredibly important.

Bruce: There are individuals who you can tell are really transforming. There are some people there who are in process. We know of two or three who we've really had a major impact on. They've really been able to reflect on their life and see their patterns and observe them.

You can see the men starting to understand that there is a way to deal with their impulses. Their impulse control and anger is one of the biggest things. Mindfulness is a way to notice your anger in the body and to work with it. It gives them time so that they don't just turn around and react. In the meantime, they learn a lot about what that anger really is.

We're just trying to have them work with their sensory experiences. In Buddhism, your mind is one of your sensory experiences. Your thoughts and emotions are part of your reality and the data input that triggers you. They become more patient, kinder, more helpful to their fellow inmates. We see that kind of behavior going on, making them less likely to get into trouble.

Jill: Recently there was an inmate who led a program for a long time. He invited us to come and lead the program with him. Then he had a family tragedy with the drowning of his nephew. He was in a state of mourning and didn't want to be involved for as long as two years. We kept inviting him to come back. Then one day I showed up and there he was, ready to lead the program all by himself.

Things are really beginning to deepen and to just feel like something good is going on with him. Part of it is recognizing him and honoring him as a co-leader. I think he's beginning to really trust, and so things are working out well. But it was really hard. It was really strange.

Bruce: There is a man right now who's in C Yard. It is a highly secure yard. Sometimes it's called The Hole by people, but they're in a slightly different position than being in The Hole. This man is in his thirties. He's a big, strong guy.

He started with us maybe about six to eight months ago and just came in out of curiosity. He was one of these guys who was sort of at his wit's end. He realized that if he were to go out into the world as he had been back then, that he'd be right back in prison. He wanted to see what he could do to improve things.

He comes anytime we run a program on the yard. He pays attention. He has talked about the way his ability to deal with conflict has changed, where he no longer escalates and he brings a sense of calm to conflict.

He told a great story about grieving. We're trying to introduce the men to their own emotional life. Like many of us, he was born in this patriarchal model of 'big boys don't cry.' We're the ones in control and must be in control. The only really allowable emotion that our patriarchal culture allows is anger.

He found out that an uncle whom he'd been very close with was in the hospital with multisystem failure. It looked like he was going to die, and he was really distraught. His first round of how to deal with that was to go out in the yard and distract himself. He got in the yard and played handball. Then he came back and he'd be uncomfortable again and unhappy. He did this for a while. Then he decided what he really needed to do was to just lie in his bunk and feel what was up for him—the sadness and the fear of the death or whatever it was. He did this for two straight days, staying in his cell and grieving. On the third day, something loosened and he was still not happy about his uncle's condition, but he was able to say his uncle led a good life and whatever is going to be is going to be.

This is what we're teaching, so it's such a great story for us to hear. It just gave him much less suffering and more peace. It turned out his uncle miraculously survived.

Here's another good story that just occurs to me. We had a good guy, extremely bright, who would always ask very provocative questions. He was a great storyteller and a potentially wonderful teacher too. He was disruptive. He would just interfere with the flow of the program. At one point, my wife and I decided that we needed to keep him afterwards and talk to him. We said, 'We really want you to succeed. We want you to come. We like you. We value you.' We said, 'But your behavior's disruptive.' And he said, 'It is?' We said, 'Yes, you interrupt and you take too much of the space.' He said, 'I don't think I'm even aware of it.'

He said, 'The next time when we're in a group together if I'm starting to go there, give me a hand signal to cut it off or whatever.' We did that once and that was it, so he stayed with us. He ended up writing some articles for a newspaper that we put out to the inmates. He was able to teach the Dharma in his own words. He ended up being a great success.

A lot of people think they know what this whole prison life and judicial system is like because they watch TV and they see it. It's different to actually meet the men, interact with them, see them come back, hear their stories, and see them as just humans who came up under really difficult circumstances. Drug or alcohol addiction is often part of the picture, so it gives you empathy for them. I've come to love the men I've come to know. I've come to love the effort, too, that they're putting in to transform themselves.

Many of them have been in for long enough that they've just stopped banging their heads against the wall. They realized this is useless. It's getting them nowhere. In fact, it's getting them deeper. There's a point system where they come in with a certain amount of points based on what they did, and based on their behavior in prison, the points either go up or down. If their points are going up, they're heading toward a miserable existence.

Jill: The inequities of the prison system get to you. Most people don't know that about 90 percent of all people in prisons are from plea bargains, not from trials. Plea bargains are so undemocratic and so discriminatory, so really separate from the legal system, but that's what we allow. That's in addition to the underlying issues of racial disparity, class and income disparity.

I've never felt unsafe, because no volunteer has ever been the subject of any violence. There were times when I would go into a yard to visit them one-on-one at their cell doors during lockdown. It's a little strange. Sometimes the tower guards are a little hard to find. Then it felt a little strange to be out there. Not unsafe, but just a little sketchy.

Bruce: I feel lucky to have found the prison work. I think if retirement was only baseball, it would feel hollow. I feel like I want to give back. As a physician, I reaped a lot of benefits of my profession, and my white privilege, and everything else. I wanted to really give back to the community any way I could.

Jill: I think the best thing about all of it is learning about people's humanity. It doesn't matter what they've done, where they've come from, what they're currently doing. There is a real sense that there's a human being there. I would say I get a sense of satisfaction. That doesn't happen all the time.

Bruce: I would say having had my Buddhist practice has been one of the reasons why I glided into retirement without a struggle. First of all, giving me things to do that were meaningful. Second of all, a way to frame whatever would come up for me around retirement, and a way to deal with it. Having some sort of spiritual practice I found beneficial. I would recommend it to others, but who knows? Because people need different things.

41

TRY IT AND SEE: FINDING THE IDEAL RETIREMENT

"I'll jump in and I'll work with an organization for a while and if I like it, I like it. If I don't, I don't."

> Try it and see. John shows how you can make adjustments during retirement. Retirement has not been a single answer for him; it's been a process of trial and error.
>
> His love of coaching and mentoring has been a constant throughout his life, and it has continued into his retirement. He was a sports coach, a mentor at work, and now is providing that same guidance to social entrepreneurs.

first retired in my mid-forties. I sold our company and I decided that I was not going to go back into business right away. I always wanted to be a junior high school teacher. When I sold the company, I went back to school to work on a teaching credential. In my previous work, I got used to being able to plan my time—to be where I want, when I want. I got into the teaching but I couldn't go through four weeks in a row being in the same place. I decided not to continue with that. I was that close to getting my degree and credential and then I backed off.

I struggled for a while. I didn't know what I wanted to do. I had been a volunteer for a really good nonprofit organization called Loaves and Fishes of Contra Costa in Solano County. I volunteered, and an opportunity came up for a board seat. I joined the board and eventually became chair of the board. But it wasn't quite fitting what I wanted to do.

Then I got a call from the folks who acquired our company. They said, 'Hey, we'd like you to come back for a while. We've got some problems in these areas. Interested?' I ended up going back to work and had a blast. I worked for them for about three years.

Then I went into my full retirement. I've been retired for about ten years, after retiring the second time in my early fifties. I was struggling to find something. I felt there was something missing in my life because I wasn't active enough in doing things that would help the world. I knew I wasn't as happy as I knew I could be.

Finding a match is not easy. It may take you a number of organizations. My approach was to just jump into things. I'll jump in and I'll work with that organization for a while, and if I like it, I like it. If I don't, I don't. That's the way you have to realize it's going to happen.

I was introduced to the Miller Center in 2012 by my son. Many of what the Miller Center companies work on are problems for the bottom of the pyramid, who are the really poorest of the poor. The companies are trying to make their life a little better with things like improved education, water filters, clean cookstoves, or improved small farmer productivity. They were all doing really important work with incredible passion, even in the difficult circumstances they work in.

I attended the Investor Showcase, which is a group of entrepreneurs who are pitching investors to invest in their enterprises. It's the culmination of about a seven-month program put on by Santa Clara University through the Miller Center for Social Entrepreneurship. These very short presentations by the founders of these businesses all over the world were just mind-blowing. They were able to succinctly describe what they did, why it was important, and why folks should support what they're doing. I was blown away, walking into that room. I told my son, 'Hey, get me to the guy that could get me into this program.'

We go through a process with the entrepreneur. There's a curriculum that's involved. That curriculum allows us to delve into all aspects of their business, from identifying who really are their customers to how you are going to sell to them.

I've had cases where the mission seems to be clear, but maybe it's not so clear. Recently, I saw Dandelion in Kenya. They have a successful nonprofit business providing medical services. They are worried about how much of their business they can sustain. They have an incredibly talented executive director who's really hesitant to charge her impoverished customers a small amount for certain medical practices or procedures. She knows in the back of her head that she has to charge more than she has been. By increasing some charges for services, she can expand her business and have a huge impact on her community. Charging for some services can make her less reliant on donors. For her, charging for services is like pulling molar teeth without Novocain.

Every time we jump on that subject, it's painful for her. You can sense it. As a mentor, it's important not to push how you think it's best to solve problems. The mentor needs to listen to, respond to, and potentially guide the entrepreneur to incorporate more variables into their thinking. You add perspectives in their thinking.

I try to incorporate all kinds of styles throughout the mentorship.

Sometimes I'll say, 'I know we've got a real problem there.' It may be a call or two before I get back to that point. I'm going to work around it. I'm going to ask and try and gather some information around it. I'm not going to go at it for a while because I've got to build the foundation of trust early on. I always try and do that with a little humor. Most of it is self-deprecating. Everybody loves somebody who makes fun of themselves. Then I can make some jabs at the entrepreneur.

Most of all, what I bring to these folks is the experience of having started my own business twice—one not successful, one somewhat successful. I really appreciate the struggle. The times where you lose, you're not sure you're going to make it. I can appreciate what they're going through in attempting to build their businesses. At times, there are not a lot of folks to talk to. When you can grab somebody who's willing to listen, it's really helpful and meaningful.

Coaching: that's what I really like to do. I like to coach. I don't care what it is. If it's teaching kids to play baseball, football, basketball at the local park, it's all coaching. You're teaching. You train them in some ways. You educate them. If it's working with my grandkids on how do you read and how do you count all those little things, you're really coaching them. When I work with entrepreneurs, that's what I'm doing. I'm just coaching. The same things I do, the things I love about doing that, that hasn't changed.

If there's one piece of advice I give people recently—that was inspired by the Miller Center—it's that you need to travel out of the United States if you haven't.

With the Miller Center, I get out into the weeds of what the organizations do. If they're selling cookstoves and their target market is the slums of Nairobi, I'm out in the slums. That has just really allowed me to see the world differently. I now see the world in a much different and more enlightened way, from the perspective of the social entrepreneur.

I would describe my retirement years as being maybe the most fulfilling part of my life. I'm still married to the love of my life. I have grandkids who live around the corner. And I work with a great nonprofit organization where I get to interface with lots of wonderful people.

42

DRUMMING UP SUPPORT FOR RESTORING ROTC: LEADING A MULTIYEAR PROJECT

"The initial mission was to return ROTC to Columbia University."

> Upon retirement, Ted made an organized effort to find something important and meaningful to do. His background included both corporate experience and military reserves, so he was ideally suited to lead the large project of restoring ROTC to his alma mater.

I was at a reunion at Columbia University. I signed up to say I was interested in learning more about the ROTC project. The initial mission, going back about fifteen years, was to return ROTC to Columbia University. It had departed during the Vietnam era, and over the next forty or more years could not or did not return. That led to the job I now do as the head of this nonprofit, Columbia Alliance for ROTC.

There were several reasons for the importance of the project.

Number one is just for reasons of good citizenship. We thought the university was missing out on a chance to contribute to national service in one major area. The second thing was that a lot of alumni felt disenchanted because at one time Columbia had a very large contingent of people in ROTC. In addition, Columbia had a history going back to 1919 of being very supportive of the military. The alumni were tired of being labeled, either fairly or unfairly, as anti-military. We decided to form a group to promote the restoration of the unit.

When I got involved, I saw a need for organization. They had fervor, but they didn't have nonprofit status. They didn't even have a name. I put that together. I was well aware that we needed to build a relationship with the trustees.

However, what we didn't do, we didn't burn the dean in effigy. We didn't protest on campus, blowing horns. What we did do is a lot of organizational work. I knew I needed support, and I got various introductions to people and the trustees so that I could make a firsthand pitch, an 'elevator pitch' as it is called.

Our work was instrumental because we mobilized alumni. We managed to get some money by publishing a newsletter and making the cause well known. The alumni and the New York press were important. I started getting support, both in terms of letters being written to the university and in terms of donations. I felt a hell of a lot better.

The students had a divided view. Even today we have very little contact with students. If we were on FaceTime, you would see that I have a lot of gray hair and probably look like some of the students' great-grandfathers. But I'll tell you how we got support. What we did was work through some of the supportive faculty. The faculty can be one hundred years old and the students will listen to them. The faculty's work extended to the political clubs to get support from the

Democratic and Republican clubs on a nonpartisan basis. We could not have done that as alumni.

After university approval to reinstate ROTC, there was no big return to campus with people marching and so forth. There was no glorious celebration. There was some press in New York and in the Columbia papers.

There was a lot of committee work done on the issues of implementation. That went very smoothly. There were no counterprotests. All the protests of the past basically disappeared. As we go forward, we need to recast the group. The missionary days are far behind us. What we need now is to get in a new and more distinctive role that helps the university people grow participation. We can help in various ways, but we need to plan with some of the military alumni organizations and reduce our footprint. The alumni today are very thankful that ROTC has been restored. The question now is how to get to the younger students. That's a challenge right now.

43

SERVING WHILE WORKING:
COMMUNITY SERVICE IN RETIREMENT

"My interaction is with a smile."

> Barb's work was always focused on helping people. Those
> skills were fully honed by her time in a convent, then as a
> teacher, then as an outplacement counselor.
>
> Retirement was a natural transition to continue to serve,
> but this time in local service organizations.

I stopped paid employment about two years ago, but I am doing
volunteer work for two different organizations. I never really
experienced any withdrawal from full-time work. I think because
when I was working it was a helping position, and I'm continuing
to do that in my retirement. So I think I've bridged the gap in that
respect pretty well.

I volunteer one day a week for six hours at a dining hall for
needy people, where we prepare the food and serve it. So that's one
day of very fulfilling work. The faces of the people at the dining hall
become familiar, and they're like friends to us. There's a wide variety
of people, from tiny tots to older people—some are disabled. Many

of them have great smiles on their faces, and there are a few grumpy people. I know they appreciate us being there because they tell us that on a regular basis. There's one gentleman who always comes in a different baseball hat. There are a few people who really should have some help dressing before they arrive because they are not always fully clothed. There's a little bit of everything.

My interaction is with a smile. The people notice how we're dressed, and if we get our hair cut they'll say something. They are paying attention to us.

One situation I remember was a woman who came in who obviously had some mental problems. She said she was looking for the queen, and so we knew that something was wrong. She got a little bit violent, and that was my first encounter with something like that. We were able to connect her with the police, who had to come in and take her.

My other volunteer job is working at the American Cancer Society Discovery resale shop. All the profits go to cancer research. Being a cancer survivor, this is an important opportunity for me to participate in.

The Discovery Shop that I work at is in a very affluent area, so the donations that we get are very upscale. We are able to make quite a bit of money for cancer research. My role there is to do the design in the windows and also put the clothing out and change the decor of the store from time to time to keep it interesting for patrons. One of the store managers has a really good sense of how to treat people. She makes us feel appreciated and she has just a really wonderful way about her. She seems to know a lot of the people by name, which makes a big difference for us volunteers. I don't know all the customers by name, but I do know the styles that they like and the colors that they like. So, when they come in, I will point them in a direction of something that I think they would like.

44

CHANGING THE LIVES OF AMPUTEES: A REWARDING EXPERIENCE

"It is life-changing for them, really life-changing."

> Milt has an active and diverse retirement. One of the highlights was installing artificial hands on Panamanian amputees.

I originally got involved with Rotary to do business networking. For a long time I was called a RINO, and that stands for Rotarian In Name Only. It's a guy who shows up every Tuesday or Wednesday for lunch, pays his twenty bucks, has lunch, talks to people, writes a couple of checks during the year, and supports a couple programs. I did that for probably fifteen years.

Then I started doing more, because our club was pretty active with some cool stuff. It was shortly after I retired when they asked me to be president. That really gets your hair on fire! Being president of a Rotary Club is one of the most fun things you can do. There's a lot of good work locally, regionally, and internationally.

I've done an international trip with Rotary to help attach artificial hands for people in Panama who had lost their hands in agricultural accidents and couldn't work. That was quite an experience. We went down to Panama for a week and a half to help attach these very basic hands. These artificial hands are for people who have at least three inches remainder of their arm below the elbow and this hand can be attached. It's manually adjustable. We had two big days where people came in and just showed up because of it being advertised. We helped them. We did about a hundred hands, maybe a hundred and twenty. I physically put the hands on. Then we trained the Rotarians down there and they put them on too. Then we taught people how to use them. It's pretty amazing, especially for these people who work in agriculture.

You can open and close this hand in all different configurations to hold things like a steering wheel when you need to drive a tractor. Even though it doesn't seem very high tech, it makes a huge difference—it allows people to go back to work. You can hold brooms, you can sweep, you can drive a tractor, you can use a shovel. It is life-changing for them, really life-changing.

45

RECONNECTING WITH PEOPLE: RELATIONSHIPS FOR FUN AND COMMUNITY SERVICE

"All the males on my father's side died before retirement. I wanted to make sure I was around to have some fun."

Dave has lofty ambitions for his retirement. He wanted to do what previous generations of the males in his family had been unable to do. Fun for Dave falls into two categories. He wants to spend extensive time bonding more deeply with friends and family. Additionally, he has identified certain community projects where he can build relationships and provide leadership. Dave is able to multitask both sets of activities as a way to have the kind of retirement that he is seeking.

would say this is probably the happiest stage of my life. I never thought life in one's sixties could be so much fun. Let me help you understand how I got where I am. When I was fifty-one, I planned that I would retire early at sixty-one. The reason was that no male in my family had ever lived long enough to retire. My father died at the age of sixty-three, and his father died before the age of sixty. All the males on my father's side of the family died before retirement. Most of that was due to poor lifestyle choices—being alcoholics, maybe not exercising, those kinds of things. Their plan was that they would work until they retired and then have fun. Having witnessed that, I wanted to make sure I was around to have some fun. During this period of time, my mother died, and I was close to her. I had a stepsister who is close in age to me. She was diagnosed with brain cancer and was dead within eighteen months. You never know, so enjoy it while you can.

I was the CEO of a company for seven or eight years. I ended up retiring actually at sixty-one. I had expected to phase out of my career and phase into other things. It was really the start of a new chapter. For me, the biggest surprise has been that I haven't missed the work. I absolutely loved my work, loved the industry, but I haven't missed it.

I declared this as the theme of my retirement: 'Be with people you love and go to amazing places.'

I went to the people who were close to me and said, 'Let's spend some quality time together.' It included my two daughters, my spouse, and also my sisters. My two sisters and I spent three lovely weeks in Europe. We had never spent that much together time since we were teenagers, and we really got to know each other a lot better. I organized a family reunion. That was great to see everybody. We just went whitewater rafting at the Grand Canyon for a week with some college friends. I also went to Alabama to see the guy who was best man at my wedding. For me, it was just a great way to get connected with people that were important to me and to let them know that.

Here's another concept that works for me at this stage of life that probably wouldn't have earlier. My partner, Wendy, and I have a relationship that might make someone do a double-take. She has a place in Berkeley. I have a place on the Peninsula, and then we have a place together in the city. On any given week, we're probably together three or four nights a week in one of those places. The other times, we're doing our own thing. It turns out that works really well because she has her independent life and I have mine. When we're together, we're very focused on each other. It's quality time, and there's always things to talk about and share.

I had planned to get involved in nonprofits. With nonprofits, it's thrilling to see how fast things can get done. You don't have to put something in a five-year clinical trial. You can get shit done. And these organizations need people who can get shit done. The kind of training that I had is really valuable to these organizations. Routine things to me are total revelations to them.

I've worked predominantly with two organizations. I was involved with both of them to a small degree before I retired. Both of them had approached me about being on the board of directors. I got involved with the boards and quickly became president of the board of both organizations.

One is a low-income housing project in San Francisco. We've made huge strides there, especially around getting cost under control. I laugh because one of the things that I used to be early in my career was an engineer. I've had fun going back to some of the old textbooks and figuring out how to do some of these projects. The geeky side of me hadn't done engineering in forty years. It was fun to do that stuff again. Those are parts of my brain I hadn't used in so long. When you're working with people in a low-income housing world, a lot of them don't have the same skill sets. I've learned to be very patient and have to explain and re-explain things. The toughest thing to explain to people is that in order to save money, you have to invest. They came in with a mindset that they didn't want to spend money on anything. Most of these projects we invested in had paybacks of much less than one year, which from a business point of view would be spectacular. When I started, they were adamant that they didn't want to spend money on anything. One of our advisors commented that they've never seen any organization like this completely change and have such a huge impact. It's great to feel that you can really make a difference.

The second nonprofit is also interesting. It's a school for dyslexic children in Palo Alto and goes from first to eighth grade. One of my daughters was ADHD. I understand how challenging that can be for parents, how the household can revolve around that issue, and how it is really important to get them the right education. Fortunately, my daughter is doing spectacularly well now. The founder of this school was a Stanford Business School classmate. She got me involved in the school. It's been really great to apply business techniques to help the school, build up the board, get governance.

When I apply what I call the biopharmaceutical mentality to what is done in education, I'm appalled that so many of these rules in education have not been proven. I picked up on this. No one has ever done the studies. There are lots of reasons they give for why they haven't done the studies.

I want to do a classic controlled study to show that the way we teach dyslexic students is superior to the way that it's done in public schools now. It's an expensive study. It's going to cost $10 million or more, but I think it could really profoundly change the way that kids are taught. That's the example of using some of the old learning and experience that I have in an entirely different application. It could make a big difference.

The thinking on dyslexia has changed dramatically. It used to be thought of as almost a learning impediment. Now the thinking, with the new neuroscience, is that these people are very right-brain oriented. They have creativity and a way of connecting the dots so that many of them can think really well in three-dimensional space. They lack the repetitive tasks, the left-brain stuff. With artificial intelligence, you can have e-readers that read to you. You don't need to be a super reader, and so these kids can excel. There are so many examples of people in everyday life, such as Charles Schwab, Governor Gavin Newsom, and Steven Spielberg, who got over those hurdles. I think there's a great way of teaching to get these kids to be superstars even at a younger age.

We just got accreditation for the first time ever. It's a classic start-up environment where the school has gone from zero to sixty kids in six or seven years. We now have faculty and a facility and those kinds of things.

The satisfaction from the dyslexic kids' school is different from that of the housing nonprofit. At graduation, there's a circle where the kids talk about what the school has done for them. You have to come prepared with your Kleenex, because these stories are just breaking you into tears. When most of these kids come, they've been failing in public school and they are often depressed. It usually takes weeks to two months before they can begin to open up and be open to new teaching techniques.

As I look forward, the real variable for me is health. I'll give you an example: When we organized this river rafting trip for the Grand Canyon, it was a pretty physical endeavor. I probably had three or four times more people who wanted to go but admitted that they physically couldn't. They're getting a knee replaced or had some back surgery. Something prevents them from doing something that physical.

I've always tried to take care of my body, and my cardiovascular system in particular. I've had more time to do cycling and some of the fitness things that I love to do. Wendy and I have prioritized trips to do the more physical things now. When it comes to things like significant hiking, ziplining, kayaking, or whatever, we're going to do that now.

The other thing is the mortality thing. We all think we're going to live forever in our twenties. Somewhere along the line, you realize that's probably not going to happen, but it's hard to internalize that. I've seen that with the males in my family. I have to say, there's still a bit of denial there, but I think I've had a few wake-up calls. I've seen this a lot with friends who maybe don't die per se but have some major physical problem that really restricts their life. My philosophy has been to 1) be in touch with people and let them know that you love them so there are no regrets later on, because you never know what could happen, and 2) take advantage of every day. When I wake up in the morning, it feels like every day is a Saturday now and I can do whatever I want. Usually that day is pretty well planned, but it brings me joy.

Sometimes things don't always work out precisely the way you planned them, but you just have to step back and put it in perspective. The advantage of being retired is you do things because you want to do them, not because you have to do them. When curves get thrown at you, you just have to be more resilient about that. When you're retired, you have more wisdom and experience. The other part is the financial part. Throughout my life, I've been an incredible saver but also worked on keeping the burn rate down.

I never had real role models for life when one is in their sixties and seventies. Our generation tends to be in much better health maybe than our parents' generation. For the people who are entering that age group, it's a fun time. I never envisioned what that could be, but it can be exciting. It can be romantic. It can be anything you want it to be. That's been a real thrill.

46

LIFE'S PROGRESSIONS: CHANGING THE LIVES OF OTHERS

"I'm helping this kid get his life straightened out."

> Ken has developed his theory of the progression of life. For him, that theory entails helping others who are in need, while at the same time having fun with his friends.

At this stage, I'm moving toward the end of life, and I am enjoying myself about as much as when I was in college. I have the time and the money to travel, and I have deadlines, but nothing like the ones I had working at my jobs. This is turning out to be a really fun time.

Think of your life as having four stages. Stage one is age zero to twenty, and you don't have to worry about anything because you're being pushed through life. You go to school, you go to college, you get out of college, but your parents are pushing you, teachers are pushing you. You're getting pushed through for the first twenty years.

The next stage is from, let's say, twenty or twenty-five to fifty. You also don't have to plan and think about very much because you're getting pulled through life by these forces. You fall in love with someone, you get married, you start having kids, you get a job. You're usually moving ahead in your job. You're getting pulled by these forces that just happen.

Now let's skip the third phase, which is age fifty to seventy, and go to the fourth phase, from seventy or seventy-five on. You also don't have to think about or plan too much because you're basically heading toward the end game. You're declining physically. You're declining mentally. You don't have to think about that too much because that's what's happening.

It's the third phase of life which is the only time when you have to actually plan ahead and figure out what you need to do to make yourself happy. From age fifty to seventy, usually your career has topped out. All of a sudden, your job is not providing all the great feedback it used to. Your kids have grown up and left. So you have a couple of voids that were occupying your life in the first two phases. You have to plan ahead for that phase, because you're an empty nest. You've got to figure out that third phase before you get there.

I guess the first challenge is to maintain your health. I'm pretty lucky. I have never had any serious health issues. The more you keep yourself healthy, the longer you can stay active.

Challenge number two is not overdoing having a good time. That means watch your drinking and make sure you don't start overdoing it or falling into habits that you probably do not want to have.

The third thing is to have a balance between doing stuff for yourself and doing things for other people. I'm helping this kid get his life straightened out. He never had a chance to go to college. This guy was one of my daughter's good friends in high school, and everyone else went off to college. Because of a combination of family things and financial issues, he went and worked in a pizza parlor. He was still there three years later. I just finally got fed up with him getting left behind. I sat him down and told him I'm going to send him to a full-time college. He wasn't even sure he wanted to do that, but it later came out, he wants to be an architect. When he said he wanted to be an architect I said, 'Instead of going to the community college one class a semester, quit your job and let's go full time. I'll pick up the freight for that.'

Before, I was just his friend's dad he would see me once in a while. Now I'm his mentor, and we sit down once a month. He said, 'I really want to experience being an architect at the very beginning of this.' I said, 'Okay, go to Craigslist and look at the ads, and maybe you'll see that some architect or firm needs someone part time.' He goes on the website—bingo. There's a one-man architect firm in the town where he lives, and the guy has advertised for someone to work ten or fifteen hours a week. He goes and he gets that job. Now he's going to school full time aiming toward architecture, and he's got a half-time job during school and full time during the summer.

He learns all the software and everything that architects need to do. Then he leverages that into an internship at a Top 25 architect firm in San Francisco. He's the draftsman. The next summer he progresses further with an architectural three-week trip to Japan. He's just made this steady progress. It's turned out way better than I ever thought it was going to turn out. He's well on his way. He's almost finished with college, and he's had all these incredible internships.

It makes me feel like I'm doing something worthwhile. I've got to find something else to do that's worthwhile. That's my next step—to make sure that I'm doing something good for the rest of the world instead of just for me.

PART SIX

INWARD EXPERIENCES: RESILIENCE, SPIRITUALITY, AND RELIGION

Inward experiences are acts of seeking of new meaning and understanding in our lives. In the stories that follow in this final section, the inward experience flows from some combination of resilience, spirituality, and religion.

Our inward experiences may change in these later years of life as we seek a satisfying personal philosophy. The causes for those changes might be one or some of the following mentioned by retirees:

- Retirement has given us more time to reflect.
- The approaching end of life has caused new thinking.
- We are applying our accrued wisdom and experience.
- There is a need to tie up loose ends in personal philosophies and beliefs.

Overall, we are able to spend less time focusing on our day-to-day activities and can address some increasingly important larger questions. There is a shift from "doing" to "being."

This shift to "being" can have different initial starting points from which to build. In the following stories, resilience, spirituality, and religion play an important role in the inward experiences that drive the philosophies and values of the retiree. The starting point for the mental changes may come from any of the following:

- A major adversity that has stimulated new responses. The adversity is often health-related and requires a substantial lifestyle adaptation.
- An expansion and/or refinement of an existing belief structure.
- A discovery of an entirely new belief structure.

These new inward experiences are both natural and healthy, and can be an important part of successful aging. We have the time to contemplate topics such as these:

- Reflecting on the meaning of events
- Communicating previously unspoken love to others
- Expanding our sense of community
- Making peace with our beliefs about death

This final section is a collection of stories about people whose way of looking at life and sources of coping have evolved into new beliefs. The deep emotional content is the result of these inward experiences having been so transformational to these people. Some of their stories may be outside of your usual beliefs, but can nonetheless be enlightening and broadening.

Our final story is about dealing with the end of life. The comments from the Old, Wise, Learning Still group moves the subject of end of life from a personal inward experience to an open, candid, and insightful group discussion.

Looking inward can produce some of the most profound and life-altering changes during retirement. The stories in this section provide diverse examples of how resilience, spirituality, and religion have combined in some way to have a major impact on the individual.

47

TEACHING MINDFULNESS: A PATH TO A NEW IDENTITY

"I bet I could teach mindfulness meditation. That truly was my transformational piece, creating a new identity almost."

Susan had to retire unexpectedly after a head injury. Her adjustment to retirement was built around taking a two-year course on mindfulness and then becoming an instructor. The change was like creating a new identity for her; her new outlook on life pervaded her other activities.

I wasn't planning on retiring, but I was in a pretty serious bike accident. I had a head injury. I was away from work on family medical leave for almost a year. Then I thought, 'I just can't do this to my program.' I was a professor in a graduate counseling program, and they needed some predictability. I decided that I would retire. That made the most sense for me because all the neurologists had different predictions on what was going to happen to my brain, the way I thought, and what I was able to take care of.

A year before my accident, I had gotten a divorce after thirty-four years of being married. We'd been separated for two years. I ended up in our family home, but I wasn't working. I didn't want to be in this small college town if I wasn't working.

My retirement was just one year post-accident. Even though I was still fuzzy in my head, I made this move to Portland, thinking that my daughter was also planning to move to Portland. I thought, 'I'll get there first.'

That was a really hard transition. After being a professor for thirty-two years, it was hard to say goodbye to that life. I was leaving neighbors and good friends, and this house that we had raised our children in. I had lots of losses. I will walk the Camino, which is a pilgrimage across Northern Spain. I'll have a full month to six weeks to just be with my thoughts and be prepared for this new chapter. That had felt like an important transition for me, from saying goodbye to my marriage, saying goodbye to my job, and dealing with my mother passing away. Eventually I couldn't do the Camino because of problems with my knees.

About that same time, a friend sent me an email with an advertisement for a mindfulness meditation program. She said, 'I wonder if you would be interested?' It just got dropped on me, and I thought, 'I'll give it a try.' I bet I could teach mindfulness meditation. That truly was my transformational piece.

It was being taught by two very well-known mindfulness teachers, Jack Kornfield and Tara Brach. It was a big deal because these two teachers are well-known. Both these teachers are getting older, and I'm thinking that they see this mindfulness meditation as being a good thing. They're wanting to see it expand. I was accepted to a two-year on-campus and online program. I was a student and I felt like I was getting a second master's degree. There were three hundred students in the program from all around the world. There were doctors and lawyers and housewives and retirees in the class.

Some people were teaching mindfulness, and therapists used it in their practice. There's this whole gamut.

I thought I could teach mindfulness meditation. I had never taught meditation, even though I had been a practitioner for many years. It was a very challenging program and very thorough. What my neurologist colleagues had told me was that new content was going to be the most challenging for me. I had to work really hard to get the language down. That part wasn't very easy.

We also had practicums that were observed by our mentor. We had small breakout groups, and we got feedback on several different teachings. The whole goal was not just the content, but to become a teacher. The teaching part never scared me because I felt confident. I feel like I know how to teach.

The classes that I taught were good. I continue to teach, and that part seems to come together pretty well. That truly was my transitional piece, creating a new identity almost. I really enjoy time to develop a curriculum that fits with the audience. That was creative and fun. I got to do something that I already knew I enjoyed but using the all-new content.

That was my Camino. That was a wonderful transition. It gave me something to do, lots of reflection, new ways of thinking about things, and ways to be in the Portland community. I would say that was the biggest and most helpful transition piece for me into this new chapter.

I thought the whole concept of self-compassion was incredible. There was not ever any striving. There was more recognizing what's happening right now and almost bowing to it with a thank-you. Part of mindfulness also is that there is suffering. Human beings suffer and our tendency is to want to pull away from the suffering. In mindfulness, there is this encouragement to look at the suffering. Deep reflection around what's true about the suffering allows you to transform it into joy or contentment. With mindfulness, there's this whole sense of pausing and recognizing. A simple strategy is to count to ten. You sense something beautiful and you're in that lovely place to notice that.

I was able to pay attention and really notice the things that work. There was no suffering. In fact, it was the opposite. It was lovely. My perception then started to shift. Instead of wallowing in that pain, I began to open up to see that this is also just wonderful. The balance began with the practice, and I would say I'm in a really good place now, a very good place.

I'm not a religious person, but I would call myself spiritual. I've always known I was bigger than just this body. My previous meditation was touching upon that piece. The satisfaction and the fit with a mindfulness meditation from a more Buddhist perspective is the best set for me in this time in my life.

As I was transitioning to this new city and not knowing anyone, I would take my dog and I'd walk around nearby Mount Tabor and get to know the park. Soon afterward I got an invitation to attend an annual meeting for Friends of Mount Tabor Park. I went to that meeting and signed up to volunteer at the visitor center and what they call foot patrol. I cannot tell you how satisfying those two positions have been. I started off with the foot patrol. You wear this little yellow jacket that says VOLUNTEER on the back and they give you one of those picker-upper sticks. You walk the park and you pick up cigarette butts. You get to talk to people. You're an ambassador for the park.

People were appreciative of the work I did. To be walking by yourself in this park and have people saying 'Hey, thank you for doing that' was so satisfying to me. That was a surprise.

Last week an older couple were coming through. They came in

and we just talked. Their house had burned down in the Paradise fire in California. It had taken this long to figure out where to go next. Both this husband and wife just cried with me. It was a mini counseling session. It was just this touching life experience out of the blue, it was perfect timing for them to share that. They really needed to talk, and I'm a good listener.

My mindfulness practice helps me see more clearly. I was a therapist for almost thirty years. Over time you learn to be a very good observer and you read between the lines and you ask questions. You learn to ask questions to help clients to get a little bit more insight. The gift of mindfulness helped me with my own self-compassion. I was paying more attention to myself and being kinder to myself.

The mindfulness has made me a happier person. I think I'm happier than I've ever been. Maybe that creates comfort for the people who come into the visitor center. I've been written up in their newsletter because people spontaneously write to the webpage and talk about how they felt welcomed.

There can definitely be times of loneliness, but I feel like I have tools so it doesn't scare me to acknowledge the loneliness. It's true that I get to do all these other very interesting things and be of service. I feel like I'm doing something wonderful. This stage of my life is so lovely, and I've had life experiences that are all too human. I feel like I have some tools to reframe these life experiences so that I wake up very happy. I wake up very interested in what does today have to bring and how could I live the most fully today. I think everybody can benefit from that, but especially people who are going through any kind of transition. Letting go of old patterns is hard, and moving into areas of uncertainty is hard. I think mindfulness has been really helpful to me and I think it's a good tool for a lot of people.

48

ADJUSTING TO AN INFECTION: SLOWING DOWN AND ENJOYING LIFE

"I don't think I ever would have slowed down."

> Craig had to deal with a health challenge that caused him to change his life for the better. He has an enjoyable reinvented lifestyle that may never have happened if it were not for his spinal cord infection. Martial arts continue to be an important part of his life.

B asically, I'm in semi-retirement, taking it a little easier than I used to. I had a medical issue a few years ago. This is why I've semi-retired. I had an infection in my spinal cord and they didn't catch it in time. I had to have plates and screws put in the front and rear of my neck. I was in the hospital seventeen days, and I'm on antibiotics for the rest of my life. The infection didn't come back. I passed my four-year mark.

My personal standpoint is that the good Lord maybe put me through this ordeal with my neck to slow me down. I don't think I would have ever slowed down and totally enjoyed life the way I am now unless I had been forced to slow down. What I went through forced me to slow down, and I think that was probably a blessing in disguise.

I just went from being president of a company and running the day-to-day operations to being basically semi-retired and taking rent and not running day-to-day operations in the company anymore. I'm just as busy as I've ever been, and a lot happier with a lot less responsibility. I have been enjoying it because there's just a lot less responsibility and no payrolls to make. It's so much easier to manage, and risk-free.

I've been involved in martial arts my whole life—judo and jujitsu. I still teach a class one day a week. It's pretty limited because since I went through the infection I had in my spinal cord, the pins in my neck have slowed me down quite a bit. I still have a group of students who've been with me a long time. They still want me to teach, so I'll teach one or two days a week.

In the early days, that's what kept me centered and kept me on track to do the right thing and become the right person. I think it helped me in my business life as well. I had a very good instructor and somebody I was very close to. It kept me very centered and focused.

I think when a person is young and growing up, they have these temptations that pull in different directions. Some of them might not be the best directions or the best things you should be doing. I think the martial arts helped me become successful in my life because it kept me focused and centered on what I wanted to do and who I wanted to become.

My students are all adults and they range from twenty-three to fifty. Most have been with me for quite a while, so they have some rank in my particular art that I practice. They're a good bunch of guys. My teaching helps them to stay centered. You lead by example, and I think that I honestly do. We have a place to gather and focus and work out and try to improve our mental state, our minds, and our bodies every week. It's a definite process for everybody, including myself. I think we all get something out of that.

Teaching keeps me more physically alert. I like being able to help somebody else and bring them along in something like this. I see how they can improve and build their self-confidence. That's very rewarding and gratifying to me. Yes, it really is.

We bow when we come on the mat, which shows respect for the school and the instructor. We leave our personal life off the mat. We come and we learn judo and jujitsu, and we spend our hour and a half on the mat and we learn. Then when we bow, we leave our jujitsu and our judo on the mat and we go back and live our personal lives. What we gain out of the practice and the focus on studying the art helps us in our personal lives.

There's no ego, nobody gets hurt. It's just a place to come learn and better ourselves.

49

DUAL CHALLENGES: HEALTH AND SUCCESSION PLANNING

"Before, I always had a very long-term plan and I knew how to get that plan designed and performed in the short term, mid term, and long term. Now it's not like that at all."

Henry is seventy-three. City Arborist is his "baby." His twenty-plus years of hard work and caring for his customers have built a strong reputation for this successful business.

But now his cognitive skills have begun to decline as a result of necrotic tissues on the brain. It limits how he can run his business today. At the same time, he has one more challenge before he can be relaxed about retiring. He has to find a home for his "baby." That new home has to live up to the professional and business standards that Henry has ingrained in the business. It won't be easy.

As he enters this next stage of his life, Henry reflects on his time in Iran, and also contemplates how he would adapt to retirement.

My life has become confusing. It's been different. Sometimes I do not really know whether I know where I am going. I take it one day at a time. Before, I always had a very long-term plan and I knew how to get that plan designed and performed in the short term, mid term, and long term. Now it's not like that at all. I either enjoy it or I suffer one day at a time. Most of the planning now is done with my wife. She is still very much helpful and goes about things exactly as she has done for fifteen or twenty years. She's alert, on top of everything. That is something that I have to be very thankful for, that I have such a person on my side.

I am tired. This tiredness is not physical. Every single weekend I still bike and I am physically healthy for my age. When you are in this physical emotional stage, the desire for joy changes. I'm not looking for that anymore. I'm looking for the time that I will be able to feel comfortable with me.

This disorder started to bother me and it actually came about in a very unpredictable fashion. I have a convertible, and one of my friends came to me and said, 'Can I drive this?' and I said yes and asked him where he'd like to drive it. 'Let's go to Half Moon Bay,' he said. On our way back, he hit a very large buck. I ended up in the hospital. They had to do a CT scan. When they did this, they saw—totally unrelated to the accident—that there are patches of necrotic areas on my brain. So that car accident actually led to this new understanding about my brain. Then everything changed. Knowing your weaknesses, you make different decisions, and that's exactly what I did.

I'm happy and still actually functioning, and physically I'm okay. I'm still really enjoying seeing people and spending time with them. It's not as fun as before, when I was healthier.

Either you have to give up or you have to fight. I'm just trying to really be positive. I have my moments, but I try to be positive. As far as the financial part, with retirement always the most important part is how are you going to retire. Fortunately, we're not going to have financial difficulty. Of course, we may not be able to have the quality of living that we enjoy now, but we're not going to have any problem.

You build up a reputation by really working hard and staying on a consistent course. In my view, it is very important for me to have both horticulture and business skills. Just put myself in my customers' shoes. If someone comes to me to help them with their trees, what do they expect really? They expect someone to come who knows the trees and knows the problems and can help the customer and help the tree. That level of expertise requires some formal education and field experience. You cannot just bring any old guy who can hold a chainsaw.

I am busy, but not as much as before. I'm not that much involved with the nuts and bolts of the business operation. Honestly, I can't, because I'm not as alert and energetic as I used to be. I'm just trying to stay within my ability to maintain the business. I spend at least five or six hours a day consulting.

I am a little bit uncomfortable when it comes to report writing because of the disorder that I've developed. Sometimes I can't put my mind together, and there is a lapse in coherent thinking. I am trying to avoid getting involved in a very complex project that requires my absolute attention to the details. I'd rather accept assignments that are not that complex. When you do have a little bit of hesitation as to what you are doing, it makes it less enjoyable versus when you are at the top of everything and your faculty is really there.

I love to see people. I love to work with people. That is the best part of what I do. In the morning I have five appointments, I go and see five people. It's the best portion of what I do because I learn from them and they learn from me. I can't replace that with anything else. Probably this is the most powerful drug for me.

I am very privileged to have developed friendships with so many prominent people during the last thirty years in California. Now they are part of our circle of friends, and even the wives see each other. It's a very unique thing for me. It's rare to be able to make friends with the folks you're working with. But this has been nice. You don't just go there to make money. I value those friendships very, very much.

Sometimes the trees are the target and the destination. In most cases, the tree turns out to be a vehicle. The joy of interaction with the people is probably the most enjoyable part of what I do. It's really wonderful.

I have thought about the future of City Arborist many, many times. City Arborist is not Henry, but indeed it is.

That is the problem. If Henry is not there, then City Arborist is not going to be the same company as people expect it to be. Therefore, separating myself from the business and expecting the business to perform exactly the same is really idealistic thinking.

I hired Tom, who is the son of one of my very close friends. He's helped a lot. It was then that I decided I'm going to retire and do something that I love.

The business didn't really perform the way that I planned for the short period of time that I actually totally detached myself. Tom tried hard to convince people that he is here and is as knowledgeable as I am, but people still ask for me.

Regretfully, Tom developed a physical disorder and I couldn't really fully rely on him. The plan for Tom to take over didn't really materialize. So I came back again. I started putting more hours into the work.

I don't know really how to solve this problem. I am looking for someone to replace me and maybe even become my partner. I am ready to give a portion of the ownership of the company to someone who is passionate, who is young, who is honest, and has a burning desire to really bring this company to the next level. I haven't been successful. I've interviewed many people. Unfortunately, I haven't seen those qualities that I am looking for. I don't want to risk it just because I want to retire. I don't want to run the risk of bringing someone who causes a disastrous result.

Most people who are in this business are starting from being the ground man and graduating into a foreman or supervisor. They do not have that kind of depth of knowledge about arboriculture and tree biology. I created a high level of expectation for my clients. That is the thing. I don't really want to let that go down the drain. I want to have someone who can continue that path.

I sought a merger. I tried. I tried many ways of approaching other companies. I tried to explain that by putting our resources together, and if I stay with you guys for another year or two, it's going to be a much, much better company. One person approached me from one of the larger companies. He said, 'If you want to sell, please come to me.' Ultimately, I can do that, but I'm not there yet. I would say it's a little bit of a foggy period of time for me right now as to what to do.

My wife is always telling me, 'Listen. Why are you just giving yourself such a hard time? When you are not working, you are not working. Why are you so concerned about what would happen?' I say, 'I am concerned. This is my baby. It is important.'

I'm not a wealthy person. I am okay. We don't have a problem, but I think that the City Arborist is capable of providing a financial backing to me and also generating enough business to satisfy someone who'll run the business. That is my thinking, but I haven't been able really to get this to happen. It is very hard. If I cannot find the right arrangement within the next two or three years, then there is no other way but to sell the company.

When I look at myself I always say, 'Thank you, universe.' I'm coming from a totally destroyed country, fleeing for my life and arriving here with no resources and leaving the good life behind. In Iran there was a revolution just like the one Mao had in China. They gave us a three-week ultimatum to leave the universities. If you stay, then you are going to be prosecuted—or worse, you are going to be executed. There were actually so many of our colleagues that were executed just because they were not a part of this regime. They were teaching while a different political system was in place. That is not their fault.

There is an intense belief among these clerics that the United States is behind everything that is happening in Iran. A few institutes in America are associated with all these problems. One of them is Harvard University. In 1970, the government decided to invite Harvard University to create exactly the same educational institute in Iran. They created something very unique that was exactly the same model as the business school at Harvard. All the faculty came from Harvard Business School. It had been there for only five years, from 1971 to 1976. I graduated in 1975.

They hate people who graduated from Harvard and, unfortunately, I am one of those. Everybody who graduated from that institute was considered a spy for the United States. I came here with nothing because I had to leave everything behind.

Planning my retirement activities is the thing that I have a problem with. Before, I was sure: I'm going to start painting again. I'm going to start writing music again, and I'm going to do this and I'm going to do that. In that short period that I had time to stay home more, I didn't do those activities at the level that I expected. With this brain problem, you do have a lapse of memory sometimes. Although it is very short, it affects you on the whole for a very long period of time. Every time that this episode happens, you are a totally different person for a few days, both emotionally and physically. Therefore, I learned with the help of my physicians to not really take a very large step.

I have a very good memory when I read something. I can read a book and immediately I can give a lecture. But within ten days, 90 percent of the book disappears. Even when I write something, I forget about what I have written in a very short period of time. That's very scary when you hear that, but I learned how to really live with it.

When you write something, usually you remember what you have written. I don't, sometimes. Not all the time, but sometimes. This actually started to impact my decisions. That's why, day by day, rather than thinking about five years from now, I know that it is not really rational to make such long-term plans.

50

LOSING HUSBAND AND SIGHT: A RENEWED SPIRITUALITY FOR COPING

"I feel like where I've been in these last six years has been preparing me for a certain path that just keeps opening up new doors."

Adapting his spirituality has been a continuing source of strength for Michael. In his earlier years, it helped him deal with coming out and also with separating from his wife. During his retirement, he explored additional approaches to spirituality. He used that strength to help him deal with breaking up with his partner of twenty-four years. His loss of vision at this time was an additional challenge, requiring life adjustments as well as spiritual reflection.

B ecause I grew up in the fifties, there were not a lot of people who even called themselves gay. People were just undercover and it was very negative. There was an appeal to being gay and I was drawn to it, but it terrified me. I didn't want to be a 'faggot.' I didn't want to be a 'queer.' That's the kind of pejorative language that I learned and that I think anyone growing up at that time learned.

That's one of the reasons that I married at a very young age. I struggled for a lot of years with my sexual orientation, which was something I never could talk about. Eventually, I divorced my wife and I also came out. That was after thirteen years of marriage. I had two young children.

I was at a place when I was really angry at my former wife. We were having a lot of issues and legal battles. I began to recognize that my anger and my feelings toward her were not where I wanted to be and that there was something I needed to let go of.

I began to study *A Course in Miracles*. One of the main things was about forgiveness. What the book said is that we're here on earth in order to learn to forgive. It helped me to really resolve a lot of the issues that I had with my former wife and to change this negative relationship in a very profound way. Both of us were really able to let go of the past and all of that hurt.

I look at who I was when I was in my late forties. I met the man who became my husband and we lived together for eighteen years. I think that relationship had a lot of good things about it, but it also was a reflection of my own limitations. I don't know if I was asking for enough for myself, and maybe I was settling.

My breakup with my partner was something that was unexpected. I was not unhappy in the relationship. There were a lot of things about it that I liked. He was someone I really cared about.

It was, in many ways, a happy life. Ultimately, what triggered our breakup was that he was not willing to put me first, and that's what I needed. It was pretty stunning to me, because it was so out of left field. It was hurtful and I was angry too, as you might imagine. When

I look at it now, I'm glad to not be with him anymore. It exploded a great deal of how I'd been living and perceiving my life.

I was sixty-eight or sixty-nine when all this began to happen. For me it meant recreating my life.

I think I had three choices. I could fall apart and feel sorry for myself and stay with him and pretend that everything was okay and just make the most of it. That was one choice. I clearly did not want that.

Another choice would've been to feel sorry for myself and take on a certain role. It's that poor thing that was left alone. That was another choice I did not want.

The choice that I really saw for myself was changing my life and continuing in a spiritual direction.

About this same time, I became aware that I had macular degeneration. My doctor told me that I had a particularly strong case of it. I have usable vision, but it's pretty blurry, and it's limited. I almost immediately had to stop driving. I had to give up a brand new car; I gave it to one of my children. I can see people if I'm in reasonably good light and close to someone, I can usually see their faces, but often I can't even see a person's features when I'm sitting as close to them as across the table.

It's been a limitation and I decided that I was just not going to let it stop me. I have not given in to this. It's a pain in the ass to deal with, because it would be a lot easier if I could get in my car and drive places, instead of having to wait for some kind of transportation. It's maybe forced me to slow down and look at life differently. Boy, I see how much more aware I am of other people's disabilities. I think it's helped me to keep things in perspective.

Dealing with all of what I needed to deal with was not just reordering but recreating my life. I discovered this group called Trillium. What Trillium means is that we are both limited human beings as well as unlimited divine spiritual beings. We have feet in both places. It's opened me up to fully understanding spirituality, of how I think we all got here and what we're here for. Trillium also talks about awakening to a recognition that we are both those things, both human and divine. One can awaken without having to do away with the human part. It just feels very present in how it operates in my life and in my consciousness. Trillium has been a useful path. The trajectory of my life has really changed. I see myself in a very different place.

Two years ago, I went on a Trillium retreat that was held in Thailand. I spent about ten days at this retreat. It was a little scary. I remember being at the airport and realizing that the taxi driver had left. I realized I was not in the right place. Not only could I not see the signs, but I couldn't have read them anyway because they were in another alphabet. It was scary to just not be able to see well where I was. Then people saw me struggling and someone came over and helped me. They got me to the right place, and it worked out. There were times when it got a little scary.

I just signed up for another retreat in Thailand. I found myself thinking about that experience in the airport and how I am going to navigate that this time. I guess it's a combination of just not wanting to be stopped and not wanting to let this condition stop me. Also, I think it's trusting that it'll work out.

At this point in my life, I really feel good about myself. I've been dating. I see myself all over again. Because of some of the men that I've been with, today I see myself as still desirable, still able to have a satisfying sexual relationship, but also to have a satisfying emotional connection with other men. I look at someone that I'm seeing right now, with whom I have such a different relationship than the one I had with my former partner. What I recognize is that this person coming into my life has not been an accident. It's a reflection of a lot of the work that I've done that has resulted in meeting this kind of a person.

That's just the way I live my life and see new people. It's not that they're better than the other people that I've had in my life before. I don't mean that at all. I think the people around us become mirrors. If we're willing to look at the mirrors, they become reflections of who we are. Through the people in my life, I see who I am and I see that I've grown so much over my life, particularly in more recent years.

Looking back at my life, I realize that I have stood up. I have taken stands. I have been willing to be different from other people and been willing to be myself. When I look at where I am now, it feels clear to me that I do have courage. I see myself as a full person and I'm proud of who I am at this point. I'm pleased with who I am. I have the same issues as anybody has. There are medical issues here and there and the stuff that happens just because the body gets older. Basically, I think my outlook is so much more open and fuller than it's ever been.

51

DEALING WITH THE UNEXPECTED: HOME BURNING TO THE GROUND

"I was awakened a little after two in the morning by these howling winds. I walked into the living room, which had a whole wall of glass sliding doors, and there were orange flames everywhere."

Chuck and his wife had a clear retirement plan. They bought their retirement home in the Wine Country of Northern California. They have a knack for making new friends and were soon settled into their community. Chuck was phasing down his engineering consulting business and ramping up his leisure activities.

The Tubbs fire changed all of that. The fire was a test of their resilience and their competence in dealing with new plans for their recovery. Dealing with the emotions of their loss, figuring out their new housing plans, and getting back to their retirement plans was an exhaustive and exhausting process.

Chuck's reset of his retirement included a new definition of what he wanted from his consulting business and his music interests.

We got home from a play around eleven o'clock, and we thought we smelled smoke from way far away. We said, 'Well, there's a fire someplace.' It didn't seem to be anywhere near us. We went to sleep. I'm a very light sleeper. I was awakened a little after two in the morning by these howling winds. The fire was being driven by seventy-mile-an-hour winds, which were very loud. I looked at my alarm clock, and it was dark. The power was out, which was not surprising, given the winds. I decided to walk from our bedroom to my office, where I left my watch at night. My thinking was, 'Okay, if it's near dawn, I'll just stay up and putter around. If it's the middle of the night, I'll go back to sleep.' I walked out of our bedroom and into the living room, which had a whole wall of glass sliding doors. There were orange flames everywhere. Then I realized what the smoke was that we had smelled. I woke up my wife and said, 'We've got to get out of here.' Two cars were in the garage, but they would have been hard to get to with the power out.

We had a third car, which was an old clunker SUV that wasn't in the garage, and we used to leave the key in it. We knew if we jumped in that car, we could just start it up and leave. My wife grabbed the dog and put it in the car and started the car and we went out of there. She chose to turn to the right to go toward more of a housing development. That turned out to be potentially a life-saving decision. The other direction was a shorter path to the freeway. We didn't realize it at the time, but that's where the inferno was.

We headed west toward the town of Sebastopol, where we have some good friends. We went there and we opened their gate. Now it's three o'clock in the morning and we've got to knock on their front door. I said to my wife, 'You better do this because you've known them for years, and they barely know me.' She knocked on their door. When they were awakened, the woman told her husband, 'I'm going to dial 9-1 into this phone. If I don't recognize who's at that door,

I'm going to hit the next 1.' She recognized her, of course, and they had no idea of anything about a fire because it was twenty miles to the east of them. They turned out to be lifesavers for us. We stayed in this little cottage they had for two and a half weeks until we were able to find housing.

Looking back on it, it is scary, but at the time, you have this fight-or-flight thing. We've had it explained to us that when you're in that mode, you no longer have rational thinking. In some sense, that's good because you're not thinking 'We could die here. We could die.' All you're thinking about is 'What is the next step?' The next step is to turn right here, to turn left at the next stop sign. You're just in a very mechanized mode. It's only months later when you can look back at it. That's when you realize how terrifying it should have been.

That night there were some people who weren't sure if their house was going to be destroyed or not. There was no question in our mind. Probably twenty minutes after we left, the house was in flames, I would guess.

After the fire, I was very angry. I was angry because I felt I'd worked hard my whole life, I saved money, I didn't spend it too frivolously, and I bought this house in a nice place and we didn't have a mortgage. The house was paid for. Overnight, it was all taken away from me. I was angry at the world. I thought that I didn't deserve this misfortune that befell me. I had a lot of anger.

Unfortunately, in human beings in general, and perhaps me in particular, sometimes anger exhibits itself in the wrong direction. Sometimes it shows up as anger at your spouse or anger at your pet or anger at the mailman. Sometimes when you have anger in your body, there's a reason for it, but the result of that anger is very wrong and wrong things come out. Which you realize five seconds after you say them, but the damage has already been done.

I'd never seen a therapist in my life, but I went to a therapist for a year.

We had a good insurance policy, and we had only owned the home for two years, so it was up to date in terms of its value. We got a good insurance adjuster guy. It was a lot of work on my part. I've spent the last year and a half, really. It has worked out well because we had a good guy and I had a cooperative relationship with him. Some of my neighbors have had poor results with their insurance companies. I had to make a sixty-four-page spreadsheet listing everything we owned that we lost. The first six months after the fire, it was a full-time job. At the time, my part-time consulting was at a low point, and I had a lot of time on my hands with not enough to do.

We decided not to attempt to rebuild our home. In a perfect world, we might have opted to do that, because my wife loved the layout of that home so much. We knew that rebuilding was going to be a circus, because 5,500 homes were lost. We looked at that scenario and we said, 'This looks like it's going to be a zoo to do this.' We took the approach that we were going to buy a home.

When we first moved into our new house, I had a forward-looking viewpoint. I thought, 'Well, this is our life now. This is what we're doing. Let's fix this up.' My wife still had a little bit of a backward-looking viewpoint: 'Well, it's not like the house we lost,' 'It doesn't have the same number of bathrooms,' 'This room is sideways,' whatever. It took a long time in my mind for her to become more forward-looking and realize this is how we're moving forward. This is our house now and there's not a whole lot of value left in looking back about what we had in the house that we lost.

I still do engineering consulting work. I'd been doing engineering consulting for thirty years prior to this point. At the time, I didn't know how I was going to find my next consulting client. I didn't have time to brood about that, because I was doing the sixty-four-page spreadsheet on the possessions that we lost. That literally took four or five months. In some sense, the turmoil that was injected into my life happened to come at an interesting time where it gave me something to do. I had a reason to get up every morning to accomplish something.

As I've gotten older, I've been more in demand because a lot of these companies are realizing the value of experience over youth. They can get the youthful guys to work ninety hours a week. That's no problem, but those young guys don't have the experience to know what doesn't work.

I'm in a band now that may or may not amount to something. At my current advanced age of sixty-eight, I have no interest in playing in bars till two o'clock in the morning. The bands that I seek out are the ones that play at wineries in the early evenings, or afternoon parties or something like that. I hope my music output increases. As I see engineering work winding down, my time needs to get filled with something. I am doing more things now like sitting in with musicians, which in the past I wouldn't have done because I was worried about being unprepared. Now I'm more willing to expand my horizons a little bit and maybe do something where I'm not quite so well prepared. I'll also meet more people and meet more musicians, so that I'll have more opportunities in the future.

52

POST-HEART-ATTACK REFLECTIONS: PERSPECTIVE ON AN ACTIVE RETIREMENT

"I had a heart attack about three weeks ago. I keep thinking I should gain some perspective out of this."

James retired more than ten years ago. He has had a hyperactive retirement. He works out more than two hours per day. He has won medals in the Senior Olympics and the Chinese Olympics. He is the picture of fitness.

He is down at Stanford every week learning new things. He has had leadership roles at the Chinese Museum and with his college fraternity alumni group.

And then three weeks ago, he had a heart attack. How could that happen to a guy as fit as James? Hear how James is rethinking his priorities, looking back on his activities prior to his heart attack, and maintaining his commitment to live in the now.

happened to read about the National Senior Games at Stanford. You had to qualify, so I couldn't compete, but I thought I'd like to watch it. I felt intimidated, and that there was no way I could ever get a chance to compete here.

I went and watched. You know, I can hang in with these people. I won't be totally embarrassed. I might not win, but I think I could be respectable. I looked at tennis. I just tried to survey the level of competition. As a result of the national games here, they had a Bay Area competition. I found a guy who wanted to be my partner. We weren't the best team, but he had an unorthodox style. We entered it anyway. We won the Bay Area. We got a gold medal.

Then we committed the next year again and we won again. Then we entered the state and we won a gold medal. It was sort of a thrill.

You've got to be in the top three from a state to compete in the nationals. We qualified several times, but I only went to one. These are the Senior Olympics. I always liked the idea of being in the Olympics.

I competed in the Chinese Olympics. I've actually got a couple of medals. I got a medal for broad jump and for basketball shooting. I did the broad jump, I ran the 100-yard dash and the 220, and I got smoked. I came in dead last but I was close in the 100-yard dash.

I had a heart attack about three weeks ago. It hasn't affected me physically or mentally. I keep thinking I should gain some perspective out of this, because I feel obliged to do that. I realize we're all living on borrowed time. I've got to make a point of spending more quality time with my wife and friends. We can't assume that we're all going to be around forever. What's scary is the guys that I know in my fraternity who are the healthiest guys are dropping. The athletes. One is in a wheelchair. He played for the Penn State basketball team. Another set a New York State High School record in discus throw. The guy looked like a freaking Greek god. He was a good-looking guy. He was athletic in basketball, track, you name it. He's dead. Another guy had Alzheimer's. He used to plan all the bike routes for us. Another guy was in the Nuclear Navy. These are the most athletic guys in our group—more athletic than I was. I'm just an average Joe who's just trying to stay in shape.

Some of the non-athletes are doing pretty good, actually. They're not wearing out their body parts. I guess they're enjoying their eating and they're getting their aerobic exercise just walking, because they're carrying an extra forty pounds. I have no idea. There's no secret to this whole healthy living thing.

I'm in the process of reexamining my priorities. It sounds trite, this thing about enjoying and treasuring your moments. I've always tried to be in the now. I think I have to not worry about the future so much as being in the now, enjoying. I used to take my wife for granted, for example. Now, every day is a date night. We should enjoy each other's company. I make a conscious decision to say, 'Hey, we're doing something special. We're going to Panera's for lunch.'

53

COMING THROUGH DARK TIMES: SPIRITUALITY AND A MISSION

"My mission statement is to be a good steward of my experience, strength, and hope."

Lanny's retirement has been a metamorphosis since his dark period. His spirituality evolved and provided guidance for him. He methodically developed a mission statement and used writing, volunteering, and self-reflection to further guide his recovery to a satisfying life.

'm wondering whether this is the last chapter. If it is, how long is it going to be? It feels like a last chapter. I'm still writing it. I haven't finished, for sure. I'm also not sure how it ends. I don't have the complete design. It's an emergent chapter, but it's definitely a new chapter.

I've gone through a very dark period. It was a period of loss. I've lost people who are dear to me and I've lost a relationship. I went through a rather tumultuous divorce, and all the social status and my place in the community has been sort of ripped apart. I lost my daughter. My daughter became alienated from me. That happens in 25 percent of high-conflict divorces, and unfortunately mine was a high-conflict divorce. That was really disorienting. I lost a lot of money. I just lost this life. It was a really 'lossy' period of time, so it was pretty dark. I was slogging my way through that. It was depressing both economically and psychologically and emotionally.

I was financially limping along, with not much private consulting business left from the aftermath of the Great Recession. It was still going, but it wasn't as strong as it used to be. After talking with my accountant, I decided to keep the shingle out. Instead of moving to Milwaukee or someplace in the Midwest that is much cheaper, I've said there are important reasons to stay in California.

I'm going to commit to a community. In my mind, that was an important commitment I made. Because I traveled all over the world for my consulting, I wasn't grounded in a community. This community was really supportive to me in a very lossy period. I recognized that. I wanted to commit to the community. I felt proud that I committed to the community.

I'm going to commit to this church where I can volunteer. Because of my background, I have a lot to offer. I used to be a Presbyterian minister. I had this teaching. I had the experience of being a pastor. I could empathize with the staff. I understood church dynamics because I've been in that role. Yet I was also outside. I had this whole other experience. The philosophy was that I saw that I had something to contribute to this fairly large church in the bosom of California. It was in trouble, like most churches are.

The teaching began during my dark period. I'd started doing it at a church over in Ross in Marin County. That was very, very meaningful to me because I could do it. I've learned that when you're in difficulty, when you're in loss, put yourself in a place where you can give, because that's where your joy comes from. It's to counteract the sadness and also get outside yourself. You get into this self-pity thing very easily if you don't have something to counter that. I was gaining in experience about what really brings me joy, particularly in a dark period of time.

My daughter came back into my life, and that was huge, just enormous for me. All of a sudden, my confidence came back. The sun came back into my life. It wasn't just me off on my own.

My thinking was then around what I call my compass, which is my mission statement. I wrote myself a little mission statement, which is 'to be a good steward of my experience, strength, and hope.' It's really that simple. When I go back and look at it, that's what I've been saying to myself. Stewardship is a word that is big and loaded with Christian and church-related stuff.

I need to flesh out my mission a little bit more. I've got to give it some structure. The first bucket was to keep the business open. The second bucket was volunteering at this church where I'd be super-involved. Then there was a third bucket, which I called writing. I found that that was really helpful to just maintain my sanity. Then the fourth bucket was an open bucket, which was that something might come along.

I've encountered some people who are much clearer than I have been in my life. The kind of people who are like Sherman marching through Georgia. I'm not sure a mission statement and buckets would be all that useful to them. I think I'm just a curious soul, and I have too many things I'm interested in and not enough time to pursue them.

For me, I needed something to discipline me and something that I could trust and something that had sufficient structure. I needed something to come back to, and that's why I called it my compass. The compass is who I am. It may be simply just that. It's my personality type or my curiosity. I tend to be an idea junkie. I get distracted easily in one sentence. The compass is really a product of a reflective part of a loop, which occasionally I go through. It reminds me of when I'm quiet and solitary and feeling rather serene and content. I can reflect on 'what are you doing?' and 'is it what you should be doing?'

Part of the compass is answering the question, 'Where does your joy come from?' It really comes from not thinking about myself, getting into somebody else and helping them. Sure enough, that's some higher purpose, however you would describe it. I structured the compass around that. That's what goes unspoken in the compass.

I came to that clarity during this loss period of time, which I associate with a spiritual journey. I don't think we go out looking for spiritual enlightenment, but I think the real growth comes out of pain and loss. Thankfully, I had enough theology in me to know that that's pretty much true.

I had begun writing again. The advantage of these buckets is that there are activities in some and then it dies off and then another one is here waiting for you. That's what happened with the writing bucket.

My book combined different parts of my background. I had a theological degree. I spent thirty-five years of my life facilitating R&D innovation projects in large corporate environments. The two words 'innovation' and 'theology' naturally came together. They stuck.

It's a collection of thirteen essays. I wrote each essay separately. I didn't know where I was going. It was like I needed to reconcile these two worlds in my life. They remained parallel but they hadn't come together. Here I am, sixty-five years old, thinking about my life. I was thinking maybe I'd just write these essays and then publish one.

What's been really interesting about this writing journey is I wrote for myself initially. I didn't have a target audience in mind. It was none of that. It was really for myself, to try to reconcile two parts of my life that had lived in parallel but hadn't really come together. I wanted them to come together.

Making sense to others is very gratifying. When you see the light in their eyes and they go, 'Oh, yes.' There's this recognition that's really precious to me. There is something really attractive to me and meaningful about that.

I just hung out. I lived really frugally. I had finished the essays. The divorce was now over. All the money outflows were done, more or less. I realized I could survive. I wasn't under attack. In fact, I wasn't spending that much money. I was quite happy, thank you very much. I can do this.

What I'm learning is the buckets now have turned into pipes. I have to use that image—of containers—but they're not buckets anymore. I'm starting to realize now, five years into this, the buckets aren't really buckets. They flow and they merge. That's a beautiful thing.

I think this is what Richard Rohr talks about in *Falling Upward* and what David Brooks alludes to in *The Second Mountain*. People who go into retirement are unprepared, like I was, to confront this more diverse identity, and they get intimidated, turn around and go back to work. Whoa, I can't take that. That's too much.

But it's disorienting. Who am I? Am I doing the right thing? There were times when there was a lot of solitude because I didn't have a family around me. What I needed to do, which I had done before, was a little writing and a little volunteering, and that kept me sane, kept me with a sense of purpose.

I think it was a lifesaver for me. It was a cushion. It was a shock-absorber, because I still could hang on to my identity. I think if I did cold turkey, I wouldn't have made it through the first year. I would have gone back to try to find some job just for the sake of my identity.

My best day now is much more self-directed—or at least I have much less urgency than when I was in the personal service business. Now I have time to consider and think and develop the quality of my responses. It's much more satisfying to me because it's a little bit more gentle. The pace is different. It gives me the impression that I'm able to decide what I do now, rather than react and have to do this and this.

That's a huge difference. I think it's also this volunteer work that's at the heart of it. I don't have to do anything. Fundamentally, you're not working to pay the bills and when you don't have to worry about that, I think something shifts. It's really pretty big. The good news is that you don't have to work for money. The bad news is it takes some getting used to, the burden to decide how you're going to spend your time.

54

A SECOND CHANCE AFTER A COMA: COMING BACK TO A NEW LIFE

"Is there something else you might want to be doing? I was a changed person."

At age sixty, Denis had liver and kidney failure, multiple organ transplants, and aortic valve replacement. He was in a coma and had six months of serious illness. He was one sick dude.

But he survived it. He came back. And the near-death experience caused Denis to look at how he wanted to live the rest of his life. Opportunities for community service came along, and he jumped at them, often without a master plan for how all of these activities would fit together. His spirituality also evolved and became a driving force in his life. In his leisure time he followed his interests in history, collecting, and writing.

Denis looks back at how this stage of his life has turned out. He is proud of his accomplishments, including being named Milbrae Man of the Year in 2014 for his extensive volunteer efforts.

n 2005 I had a serious health problem. I had liver and kidney failure; I had an aortic valve replacement. I was very, very sick. I had been teaching and all of a sudden I was in a coma. I had six months of serious illness. I had thirteen hours of surgery. I had a lot of downtime and the recovery period after the transplants. I couldn't do anything for six months. I had to sit in my chair and exercise and eat lots of calories.

When I got well from that, I was just turning sixty and I had a chance to sit back and reflect. I knew I could continue teaching, but I'd had a life change. The life change was, 'Is this all there is? Is there something else you might want to be doing?' I was a changed person.

It was very much spiritual. I'm Roman Catholic, but I'd been away from the church for years and years. I reconnected in a new way. Instead of going through the formulas of organized religion, I started having conversations with Jesus. I became a lector in church, so I did readings once a month, and I brought communion to the hospital patients. It was a nice, very short kind of volunteerism. It didn't take a lot of time but it reinforced these spiritual feelings that had risen inside of me at that time.

As I got well, I had a lot of time on my hands. It gave me time to think about things. I don't remember making a conscious decision to start doing community volunteer work. But when opportunities came up, I grabbed them.

My first big one was because I had experience in fundraising and development. They were trying to renovate an old scout house log cabin that was built in the fifties. It was just boarded up and it was built by the Lions Club. It was on land that was leased from the school district. Somebody asked me, 'Could you sit on this committee and help us with a fundraising development?' Eventually it wound up to be my project. I went into a room and there were twenty-five or thirty people from around the county and every constituency was involved. I was really big into organizing meetings and it just was a huge undertaking. I was asked to get it organized, and I did. I honed it down. I got us working in committees.

People began to gravitate to me because they knew I didn't have an agenda. I didn't belong to any of the constituencies or the groups or special interests. I found that refreshing. People trusted me because I didn't have anything to gain by telling lies.

I've always believed that leadership is getting stuff done through other people. I found people to be willing to help, but not quite knowing what to do. There was no tax money, no government, no big grants. We did that as a community and it was the most wonderful experience because it got people talking to each other from disparate groups. At the start of the project, they didn't know each other very well, and they're still friends today.

I look on that as a wonderful success. I was named Milbrae Man of the Year a couple years later.

After that, I began to offer my services to numerous little nonprofits. I felt my effectiveness would be in bringing my gifts to their organization and helping them get their stuff together. It's a wonderful place to be. It really is. I am on the board of the ombudsman. It's a state-mandated agency which responds to senior complaints in skilled nursing facilities. I've been doing that for a while now and I'm president of the board. I've also been involved with the Milbrae Community Foundation, which is a local fundraiser for all things Milbrae, and the Milbrae Education Foundation, which is a very important piece of educational funding. I've been involved with the Boys and Girls Club since the beginning of the scout house project.

I'm a phone call away. I'm sort of a fixer now. I put people in touch with other people. That's really rewarding because you're being asked because that person trusts you to help them. You're honoring colleagues who you know can do the work. You put the two parties together and they work it out. I've seen more and more success in doing that kind of thing.

The common theme is that these are all nonprofit organizations that are about the community. I've learned since I've been on the school board that we're not a closed village. We're not just the schools and the parents. We have to be integrated into the whole community, and that's how we raised half a million dollars. I see the connection of people doing good and I'm glad to be a part of that. I wish I had more time to be more involved, but I think what I provide to them is appreciated, and I hope it is helping.

As I get older, I find myself slowing down a little bit, but to fill the vacuum, I've gotten back to some of my hobbies. I'm a collector. I collect everything. I have a huge coin collection, especially English Tudor coins, which are lovely. I collect memorabilia. I'm very much a fan of the sixties. I even have a 'Jefferson Airplane Loves You' pin, which is an original.

I teach some Human Resource Management courses. I've kept my hand in because I enjoy it, but now I'm doing it mostly online. Although I'm somewhat tech-savvy, I wasn't prepared for these platforms. I think the hardest part has been losing touch with my students.

I've found that I really want to write. Back in 1977, I was at a flea market in San Jose and I picked up this old autograph album from State Normal School. There are these flowery initials, EMV, and everything is directed to Emma, in a town that originally was called Fiddletown. I started going up to Fiddletown in the gold rush country. I brought the autograph album with me and I started knocking on doors. I was referred to Emma's great-niece. So, four o'clock in the afternoon, I knock on the door, a nice lady answers, and I show her the album and she says, 'That's my aunt Emma.' This is the connection. It turns out that Emma married a man from San Jose and became a schoolteacher. They had a very adventuresome life. It's an exciting story and it's a sad story, because her husband died thinking she was having an affair.

After my visits in Fiddletown, we had some experiences that were somewhat paranormal. Things would happen in the house. It made us think there was a presence. I never felt fear, but I certainly felt Emma wanted to be known. I've been wanting to write about Emma, and I finally got a chance to at least get the material organized and up to date. Now with the internet, I'm finding even more stuff, all these years later.

I often think now, as I'm getting older, I wish somebody had told me when I was forty what it was going to be like when I was sixty. They don't tell you that things change, and you have to be ready for that. At some point you're going to retire, either by force or by voluntary action. Get ready, because your life isn't over—so use the time.

55

DEALING WITH END-OF-LIFE ISSUES: FRIENDS BEING FRIENDS

"We are all concerned about the rest of our lives and how we're going to approach it, what we're going to do with it, what we think about it."

OWLS are Old, Wise, Learning Still. It is a group of five lifelong friends who have a long-term relationship of love and trust and understanding. They have met once a month for the last two years to explore aging and end-of-life issues. Three of the participants in the group are interviewed here.

Sally: We've known each other for thirty years. We're all teachers from the same school. We would go off on camping trips together. We have meals at each other's houses. We've been together a lot. We're all seventy-plus-year-olds.

Jane: It's a great group. We've known each other since our children were little. We have not only the history of knowing our families, but sharing the same philosophy and values through the school where we all taught. We're all at a little different place personally in our lives, but we're all facing aging bodies, aging spouses. We discuss everything.

Jill: Our purpose is really a desire to put dying and death on the front burner. Our culture has a strong aversion to being open to decline and death. The purpose of opening to dying is that it informs how we live.

It's gotten more and more comfortable. The other thing is, I did not want to be the leader of the group. I wanted it to be all of our group—that we would take turns deciding on what we would read and what we would do and maybe leading the discussion on how we would do it. I didn't really have an agenda for how it was supposed to be. It's growing and deepening. I'm very happy about that.

Jane: We just talk about where we are and where our families are and what we face, including death. We're not shy about looking at any of these issues. I probably have more to deal with because my husband's older and he has had some health issues. There's been some really close calls. That's been helpful for me to be able to talk about it, but I think other people have learned that this is something they will be facing.

Sally: We all have children who are at the stage of life where we're free from the daily grind of being their parents. We all worry about different aspects of their growth and their take on life, so we share that frequently. Jill's been our guiding light. The rest of us just bring in our own take on what's going on. We share what we're dealing with on a pretty regular basis, and how that husband's doing or how we're doing. It's very much give-and-take. Jill is a great thinker. We are all active participants in the discussion and each of us expresses our views.

Jill: I don't even want to call any of these spiritual practices, because that's just a label. I wanted to know if these old ladies like me wanted to explore issues of aging and dying, and they did.

Sally: It's just a spiritual aspect of understanding your soul and where that takes you, and you have to be open for enlightenment or just, I don't know, guidance.

Jill: It's a big part of Buddhist practice to contemplate, to understand that this life is really precious and it's also fleeting. What happens in Buddhist practice is you look at it, you look at it very intentionally, and not in a morbid way, but in a way that helps you understand more, as much as you can without going through the process. Everything is changing all the time, including you, and every day you are getting a little closer to the end, so accept it, it's just part of nature. That's all. It's making us understand we're actually part of nature too. We're born, we grow, we decline, we die. There's nothing you can point to that doesn't do that.

Jane: We read *The Five Invitations* by Frank Ostaseski and we went through that. I remember one of the things that really stood out for me was to really listen and respect where that other person is. I know I'm the cheerleader and sort of like, 'Let's go, let's do this!' Well, sometimes people just aren't there with you. They don't want to do that.

Jill: *The Five Invitations* was written by a Zen priest. It was really written in layman's language about a lot of issues of aging and death. It is beautiful. So we started with that and we've gone on from there and explored in a lot of different ways. Different people bring things to read and we've watched movies and videos and read articles. That's how we've been approaching it. In a certain way, we're just beginning to dive in.

Sally: We read *The Sage's Tao Te Ching*. It has wonderful little poems that are just really pertinent to this time of life. We talk about everything. We cry, we laugh.

Jill: One of our most memorable meetings was a movie, a documentary that we watched together and that has a lot of power just because of its form. The emotional response was right there for all of us. It was really beautiful. That stands out but it doesn't mean that the other ones weren't really vitally important.

Sally: Well, one of us, whose husband is just so very ill, they had a whole family get-together because it was confirmed that he was dying. She related the story about how it was so wonderful telling him the magnificence of his life in his presence. Then he woke up the next morning and he said, 'I'm fine.' He's still going on an uneven line, but it is generally up.

Jane: It would be hard to just bring in diverse people who might be interested in the topic but have no history. There needs to be a commitment to be open and honest and to not be afraid of some difficult subjects. And sharing common values.

Sally: People in a group like this need to be good listeners as well as pretty comfortable with sharing their deep feelings. Starting off with some good literature would help to give you focus.

There are five of us. It's ideal. I think it's something that everybody should have an opportunity to do. It just makes you open windows to things that you didn't even think about. With the five of us there, it just ricochets back and forth. It's lovely.

Acknowledgments

GENEROUS HELPERS OF A
FIRST TIME AUTHOR

When I have seen the long list of acknowledgments for other books, my first reaction has always been one of surprise. Why are so many people needed? The author writes a book and then a few people help improve it and a few others help to get the book published and distributed. It should be pretty simple.

I could not have been more wrong. It's not simple. Getting a book published these days is a long and winding road. It takes a lot of patient help from a long list of people who are willing to do favors, just because they are nice people. It's especially daunting for a first-time author, trying to understand a business that is dealing with a record flood of manuscripts seeking to be published. Said another way, I was pretty dumb about the subject, and there were lots of others competing for publication. A remarkable group of people offered to help, even if I was asking dumb questions.

The essence of *Shifting Gears: 50 Baby Boomers Share Their Meaningful Journeys in Retirement* is the stories. There are some truly amazing stories about retirees reinventing themselves during this stage of their life. The book is nothing without those stories as a starting point. The interviewees graciously agreed to a face-to-face or phone meeting, often for more than an hour. Follow-up interviews for clarification or expansion were a frequent occurrence. Lots of these people also gave referrals to people they knew, who then provided some of the best stories in the book.

The part that I am most grateful for is the candor and openness of the interviewees. They wanted to share their story, emotions and all. They told about the activity, what it meant to them, what was going through their minds at the time, and what lessons they learned.

Many, many interviewees also became partners in the decisions about the book. The book is aimed at boomers. Who better understands how a boomer thinks, and what they would like in a book? Many participated in the title selection, the cover design, and suggestions for improving the book. You will see pictures of several of them on the book cover, to give a realism to the promise of the book.

Here's the list of interviewees. Thanks for providing your content and all of the other assistance you offered along the way.

Jim and Nancy Crampton, Jack and Sally McElravey, Dan Ghiorso, Dave Pritchard, Vicki and Rick Eigenbrod, Deb Phairas, Chris Christoffersen, Paul and Judith Janofski, Paul Sakamoto, Ag Meeks, Henry Ardelan, Dennis Symanski, Bruce and Jill Hyman, Susi Van Wickle, Linda Bell, John de Castro, Suni Petersen, John Dye, Denis Fama, Lanny Vincent, Jane Krejci, Peter O'Riordan, Dave and Eleanor Yick, Chuck and Sara Geber, Brad Berman, Stuart Brown, John O'Keefe, Chuck Bell, Rich Swanson, Bill Bergerson, Eleanor Burke, Greg Gudorf, Andy Haiduck, Butch Morgan, Dave and Ellen de Simone, John Haiduck, Dorothy Butts, Dick Schiendler, Tom Kreuser, Dano Michaud, Donna Domino, Milt Smith, Craig Bell, Larry Briggs, Don Elliott, John and Ellen Gladys, Michael Outwater, Joe Boudreau, Pedro Morales, Ted Graske, Maurice Jacobsen, Julia Smith, Mike Kalbrier, Beau Walker, Kip Acheson, Steve Weeks, Jan Reese, Gus and Milo Hamilton, Micah and Myiah Thomas.

Selecting the best content for the book turned out to be one of the most difficult tasks in the whole process. I had done seventy-five-plus interviews, and the average transcript was ten to twelve pages long. Eight hundred pages was clearly out of the question. Even a first time author knows that.

Slimming down the content involved two elements. First was selecting which stories to keep and which ones should go. There's so much good stuff. How could I cut it? In part, the solution was to look for duplicates. There were, of course, no exact duplicates, but there were stories that had strong similarities. Eliminating the duplicates reduced the number of stories.

So now we were down to fifty stories of ten to twelve pages each. The second part of the selection process was to extract the best out of each interview. Many of the interviews covered multiple topics. Picking out the best elements of each interview provided further shortening. At the end of that process, we had a book that was going to be the right length of about two hundred fifty pages. Mission accomplished on getting to the right length.

Now, how about my guilt? How can I face the interviewee who either did not make the cut at all or whose favorite part of the story was axed? I start facing up to my guilt by giving the above explanation to the interviewees and asking for their understanding.

Much of the material that did not make it into the final book did make it into social media and blogs. The richness of the content from so many good interviews created the ability to support an active and interesting presence on social media. Let me give you an example. Every day I go on two retirement discussion groups on Facebook. Every day there are questions about some aspect of retirement, asking for comments from the experiences of the others on the site. Almost every day I have a reply that responds to those questions with one of the experiences of one of the interviewees. Often that reply stimulates lots of further dialogue and discussion that is helpful to the person asking the question.

I had heard a lot of horror stories about transcription of interviews. I started by buying a handheld recorder that had gotten spectacular reviews. After recording the first interview, I sent the recording out to a few transcription companies to do a test drive. Every one of them came back to me to say the format of the tape needed to be modified in order for them to transcribe. I emailed them all to ask what to do. Within ten minutes I had a reply from GoTranscript saying they could make the changes that were needed, no extra charge, and no action needed by me. That was a standout response. I decided to go with them based on the quality and speed of their response. A few days later, it occurred to me that the CEO of GoTranscript really should be told what a great person he had working for him and how that caused me to give them the business. I sent an email to my contact telling the story from my perspective and asking that my contact pass it along to the CEO. The reply was simple: "I am the CEO."

Recordings were done in a lot of strange places, often with background noise, sometimes with mumbling or accented interviewees. Somehow the transcription service managed to figure out what was being said. I was particularly impressed when weird proper nouns were in the conversation and they showed up in the transcript spelled properly, obviously after someone had looked them up.

A very helpful partner during the editing process was Julia Pastore. She is a freelance editor, whose previous experience involved working at three of the Big 5 publishers. After I had done a first edit of the interview transcripts, she went through every one of them and made valuable comments about how the story played to her. Was it interesting? Was it clear? Was it unique? What was the most compelling part of each interview?

She also helped me navigate through the question of voice. My interviews with retirees were conversations—lots of slang, run-on sentences, pronouns with unclear antecedents. We wanted the output to retain the conversational tone, but we also needed to be sure a reader could make sense of the printed word.

Julia had just the right characteristics to make working together productive. She was kind and patient, but there was never a time that I doubted what she really thought. If something was bad, she found a way to nicely be insistent. All final errors in those judgment calls are mine, but Julia was always there in a constructive and indispensable way.

It was clear to me that getting a book published these days requires a working knowledge of how the industry works. In the early days of the process, there was a course taught at Stanford called From Writer to Author: Navigating the Twisty Path to Publication. This online course, taught by Malena Watroux, was an invaluable starting point. Each week, there would be guest speakers along with Malena, helping us understand the ins and outs of how this big puzzle all works.

The next big learning came from attending the San Francisco Writers Conference, back in the days when face-to-face conferences were still possible. Under the leadership of Laurie McLean, this conference was like drinking from the firehose for me. It is an organization that really cares about helping first-time and experienced authors get to their next level, and it puts together a jam-packed few days of opportunities to learn and to network.

In parallel with these activities, I sought the help of several author friends and referrals. They each gave generously of their time and expertise to reduce the number of dumb things I might do—in completing the book but also in figuring out how to get it published and promoted. Those authors were as follows:

Dan Welch, who is the author of *Race for the Mind*

Sara Zeff Geber's most recent book is *Essential Retirement Planning for Solo Agers*

Tom Sanger's most recent book is *Without Warning*

Patty Kogutek, author of *A Change of Habit*

Rick Eigenbrod, author of *What Happens When You Get What You Want?*

Monica Tesler, author of *Bounders*, a young adult sci-fi series

They each helped in their own way, but all were patient and candid about the lessons they have learned in their process. I would not have gotten to this point without their advice.

As we began to build a platform of people with interest in the book, we worked with Linda Lee on the design of a website.

As a novice in social media, I had a buddy who was my Twitter coach. Harry Van Wickle got me off to a good start in building an effective platform.

Regular weekly follow-up on each next step came in a Friday Zoom call with Tom and Nancy Kreuser and Jack and Jan Reese, all of whom offered the perspective of this generation of retirees.

George and Debbie Flammer helped a lot along the way. In addition to being the photographer of the author photo, George provided the idea of introducing each chapter with a quote.

Another helpful source of information was BAIPA, Bay Area Independent Publishers Association. This group provides a safe place to talk about the challenges facing authors and provides speakers, resources, and shared experiences to deal with those challenges.

Susan Williams is the Founder of Booming Encore which is a website and social media platform with a continuous flow of new thinking about this generation of retirees. She provided continuous help and advice along the way.

Substantial business and logistical help came from Bublish. Their expertise is to help first-time authors through the process of self-publishing. They take care of things like cover design, editing, interior layout, distribution, and marketing. As I write this acknowledgment, Bublish has been helping for about four weeks, and has been useful and insightful and not hesitating to challenge elements that need more refinement. They were instrumental in selecting the final title, after careful analysis on their part. Their cover design does an excellent job of reinforcing the promise of the book of multiple diverse stories. Their editing process has been superb and exceeded my expectations. It was not just about fixing errors, but also improving choice of words to tell a better story. Although there is a lot more help to come from Bublish, their excellent start bodes well for our future productivity together.

Last and certainly not least is a family that all pitched in to provide substantial help along the way.

Our Seattle daughter, Beckie, and her husband, John, were frequent reviewers of titles and cover designs. Gus and Milo, our grandsons, participated in one of my first interviews and gave the grandkids' perspective on retirement, which appeared as a guest blog at adventureswithgrammy.com/blog/retirement-the-grandkids-view.html. Twelve-year-old Milo even contributed an idea for the title, which was *The Life of Seniors and How to Come About Retirement and How to Deal with Being Old.*

Our Lafayette daughter, Melissa, and her boys, Nick and Ty, were frequent contributors to idea generation, review, and brainstorming. Melissa took on the daunting task of almost being a chief operating officer of the project. She provided lots of great advice and also was hands-on in working through a lot of the logistics of our multiple activities. She was instrumental in keeping my sanity as parallel deliverables needed to be completed, often requiring technology skills that were far beyond my capabilities. Things like website design, use of Dropbox, etc., are not made for seniors, but Melissa patiently got me through both the tasks and the technologies.

Dasher, our sixteen-year-old hobbling yellow lab, was a source of constant companionship through the book process. The writing activity was isolated in a writing room, away from human contact, and with a need to concentrate. Having a loyal dog looking you in the eyes provided a much-needed break in the action.

Finally, and especially, the love of my life, my wife of fifty-two years, was there making it possible for all this to happen. Barb was kind, patient, and understanding, and went above and beyond the call of duty. With COVID restrictions, plus the California fires, she was sheltering in place a lot. I was not much of a companion when I was locked away working on the book. Never was that a problem for her, and her patience never appeared to wear out. She redefines the word "supportive."

Made in the USA
Las Vegas, NV
01 September 2021

29255073R00154